*Where Did **That** Child Come From!*

For Leslie, Jason and Darla

Where Did **THAT** Child Come From!

Why Some of Our Children Turn Out So Different From Us
and
What The Answers Reveal About Our Parenting
and Ourselves

David B. Cohen, Ph.D.

Octavo Press
An imprint of Templegate Publishers
Springfield, Illinois

Published by Octavo Press
An imprint of
Templegate Publishers
302 East Adams Street
Post Office Box 5152
Springfield, Illinois
62705-5152
217-522-3353

templegate.com

ISBN 0-87243-258-0
Library of Congress Control Number: 2003107734

Contents

Introduction
Four Big Questions

Strange, isn't it, how our children wind up so different in so many ways from us and from each other. Some children grow strong, even despite many disadvantages and negative expectations. A little kid who doesn't seem all that motivated or self-confident turns out to be a good husband and successful businessman. A troubled adolescent settles down to married life and adult responsibility. A gifted child becomes an accomplished, high-achieving adult. What pleasure parents experience when children show such positive developments.

Alas, other children flounder or fail, despite many advantages and positive expectations of loving parents. A talented child winds up a failure while a well-behaved child winds up stealing cars or getting hooked on drugs. How disappointing for parents when a child becomes increasingly self-centered, misguided, mean spirited, or mentally ill.

Initially, we all have fond hopes and great expectations. Then reality sets in and we find ourselves amazed at how things turn out. Who would have predicted such outcomes, the good or the bad? Who or what could have caused or prevented them?

We parents have many roles: teacher, advisor, nurturer, policeman, therapist. Our obligation is to civilize our children while providing opportunities for them to develop their talents. We insist on good conduct and socially appropriate behavior. We teach them skills, help them overcome anxieties, and promote their self-esteem. We share the symbols and values of family and culture. We do all this, and more.

Yet so much of what we try to make happen doesn't seem to sink in. How curious, when we bother to think about it, and important too. For it goes straight to our key question about why our children turn out the way they do. To see what I'm driving at, think of parenting as something like nutrition.

For physical survival, all children need nutrition. Beyond the basics that all normal parents supply, however, the type of food—American, Asian, or Italian, for instance—probably will have a minimal effect on a child's physical development. Perhaps even occasionally deficient nutrition will have no more lasting effect than a bruise or cut that leaves no scar.

Likewise for psychological survival, all children need parenting, but what about beyond the basics that normal parents provide? Perhaps our style of parenting—strict or lenient, for instance—doesn't affect our child's personal development nearly as much as we think it does. Perhaps it matters surprisingly little to how our child turns out.

If this seems unreasonable, I hope to convince you otherwise. In the meantime, here's a novel suggestion. Try imagining your child raised from birth by adoptive parents yet turning out remarkably the same in many ways as if you had raised them. There's good reason to think it might be so, if only because all of the striking anecdotes about genetically identical twins raised from birth by different parents yet displaying remarkable similarities and experiencing wondrous coincidences. For example, in a group of about 200 such identical twins reared apart, psychologists discovered coincidences such as these:

* two "dog people" who either showed their dog or taught obedience school
* two who typically wore seven rings
* two who had each been married five times
* two captains of volunteer fire departments
* two who left little love notes around the house for their wives.

The most amazing combination of unlikely coincidences probably involves Jim Springer and Jim Lewis. These identical twins were separated at one month and adopted by unrelated working class parents. Yet despite their different upbringing, they wound up surprisingly alike in their personality, intelligence, tastes, preferences—even quirks.

Both twins used the same rare toothpaste (Vademecum), shaving lotion, hair tonic, and cigarettes. They had the same kind of job and enjoyed the same hobby. They even had the same odd behaviors, for instance, entering the ocean backwards, but just up to the knees.

Both twins were compulsive fingernail biters and both suffered tension and/or migraine headaches. Both drank Miller Lite, chain smoked Salem cigarettes, drove Chevys, and vacationed in Florida. Both had training in law enforcement and experience as part-time sheriff's deputies. Both enjoyed mechanical drawing and stock-car racing. Each had built a circular bench painted white that surrounded the base of a tree in their yard.

Not all identical twins raised apart show so many unlikely coincidences. It's just that fraternal twins who share only 50 percent of their genes rarely show any such coincidences despite growing up together. This key difference between fraternal twins and genetically identical twins reveals two facts of life. One is the power of nature to make genetically related children similar and genetically unrelated children different. The other is the power of nature to limit parents' influence on how their children turn out.

Ignoring these two facts of life can become a serious problem when parents risk pushing their kids too hard and too far. For example, some parents with an unrealistic belief in their power to determine their children's development can wind up chaining the child and themselves to a treadmill of goals and schedules. It's as though they are driven to prove their own worth by their children's success.

What gets lost in all this is a proper humility regarding a parent's power, given the biological potentials of each child that limit such power. Losing sight of this fact of life, we parents can wind up taking too much credit for the good things that happen while accepting too much blame for the bad.

"We carry so much guilt, blame, and shame," said one parent sadly, yet without bitterness. "People think we must have done something terribly, horribly wrong to make them act that way." This common belief in parental responsibility is understandable. It's what hundreds of "how-to" parenting books are all about. Moreover, it's something professionals have promoted for generations.

In *Dr. Spock Talks with Mothers*, for example, the famous baby doctor writes, "How does a person get to be a psychopath? Generally speaking, it happens because nobody loves him the first few years of his life." This kind of parent-blaming may sound reasonable, coming as it does from professionals who are right about many important things. Unfortunately, such professionals can be wrong about other equally important things.

Sure, bad behavior and bad parenting are related. But does this relation mean that normal children get turned into psychopaths by unloving parents? Perhaps normal adults get turned into unloving parents by psychopathic children! Same relation, yet a different explanation, and worth considering given how many traits of a psychopathic personality stem from a child's biology.

Clearly, we need to distinguish between responsibility for good parenting and responsibility for how things turn out. Responsibility for good parenting is unquestionably ours. Responsibility for how things turn out, however, is *not* unquestionably ours, as we will see. My point is simply that appreciating the difference is essential if we are ever to understand what our parenting and children's development are all about.

Increasingly, professionals are now saying as much, some rather forcefully. For example, psychiatrist E. Fuller Torrey writes, "I doubt there's been a time in history where there has been the obsession with child rearing that we have now. Especially from the World War II era on, parents have had an inordinate fear that any little thing they do may permanently misshape their child's psyche." Likewise, psychiatrist Sidney Walker III writes:

> Talk shows regularly feature psychiatrists who explain why John suffers from anxiety (his father was overprotective), why Jane abuses drugs (her parents subconsciously rejected her), or why Tom is a mass murderer (his father was cold and unfeeling—or perhaps overaffectionate and threatening) . . . . What's more, according to many psychiatrists, even the most minor of parental faults—cutting the apron strings too late, assigning too many chores, or attending too few Little League games—can lead to disastrous consequences.

The message is mostly nonsense. Yet too many parents seem to accept it, which is why parent-blaming is such big business. It's why so many critics including Torrey and Walker are speaking out. What's to be done?

My best advice is that we parents pay less attention to fashionable opinion and more to solid evidence. Only then can we find out just where our influence is greatest, as well as where it is weakest. Only when we get a lot smarter about how things really are can we then truly appreciate how much certain forces outside our control limit what we can hope to accomplish.

Yet for all this to happen, we'll need answers to the deepest questions we can ask about our influence:

• *How real is it?* Some of our influence is certainly real. We manage our children's behavior in the home, we stir up strong feelings and lasting memories of family life, and we shape their social conduct. However, some of our influence will prove to be illusory, that is, where our child's heredity rather than our efforts proves to be the stronger influence. Still, because much of our influence is real, our next question must be:

• *How enduring is it?* We parents can make our children do all sort of things: take gymnastics, study hard, do chores, be kinder to their siblings and more considerate with their friends. Sure, but how much of all this sticks for a lifetime? How much does it turn a child—*our* child—into a more responsible, intelligent, confident person? Likewise, how much does poor parenting cause a child to become a less responsible, less intelligent, or less confident person? Whatever the answers—however enduring our influence—our next question must be:

• *How strong is it?* How strong is our influence relative to other influences from genes and prenatal life in the womb to peers and popular culture outside the family? As always, answers will depend on what we are talking about. For some traits, such as those involved in social conduct, our influence might be large. For others, such as IQ or risk for severe mental illness, it might be small. Whatever the answers—however strong our influence—our next question must be:

• *How controllable is it?* How much do the real effects of our influence reflect what we expected and worked hard to make happen? We may insist on, say, sobriety or civility, yet provoke the opposite. Some things that work well with one child may work poorly with another. All this makes us wonder: Who has more control over our influence, our children or us?

Whatever the answers to these questions prove to be, we must be honest with ourselves. How much do we really care about what the evidence tells us? Assuming we do care, then how much will

11

the answers change our views and make us better parents— smarter, wiser, less guilt-ridden?

One thing is certain, though. None of the new insights into the nature of our children's development can deny that good parenting is better than bad parenting or that we are responsible for trying to make our children behave better.

Rather, they reveal what many parents already appreciate. Forces outside our control—the biological as well as the social— can challenge our expectations, frustrate our best efforts, and limit our power to influence how our kids turn out. To appreciate even better how much and why this must be so, I suggest we begin with one of life's great mysteries.

PART 1

HEARTS AND MINDS
Children's Impact on Parents

Chapter 1
Learning the Rules

Our exploration of parenting and child development begins with the strange inner world of a child's mind. For in that wondrous and spooky realm—so impulsive, so self-centered, so inventive—we discover deep differences between what we have been teaching and what our children wind up learning. Those differences raise a key question: Just how much does the power of the so-called formative years come from our children rather than from us?

The likely answer: Quite a lot, if all the scientific findings and personal anecdotes are any indication. To appreciate what all this means for us, I suggest we begin with one of my favorite anecdotes, a wonderful story told by psychologist Selma Fraiberg about a little boy who would soon be flying to Europe with his parents:

Initially David was excited about the trip. Then, gradually, he became subdued, even despondent. When pressed for an explanation, the tears came as he blurted out his secret. "I can't go to Yurp. I don't know how to fly yet!"

Clearly, David was confused about a couple of other things. First, he assumed his parents could fly but had not yet taught him this advanced skill, which to him meant that his parents would fly off leaving him stranded on the front lawn. Second, while he knew about airplanes as little things that move in the sky, he hadn't figured out people fly in them.

"Here is a little boy," says Fraiberg, "who speaks our language so well that we can confidently discuss European trips and travel plans with him, but we discover that, after all, we are not speaking the same language. In the fantastic world of a two-year-old, all things are possible, and a mother, a father, and a little boy will assemble on their front lawn one morning, flap their arms and take off for a continent across the sea."

A child's preoccupation with security could explain how even a much loved three-year-old might nevertheless have a nightmare about being abandoned by his parents—like little David imagining his parents flying off to "Yurp" without him. Such a "foolish" dream may seem senseless to fretful parents. Yet it makes good sense to anxious children, for it explores a question that is vital to them. What if the world were *not* so comfortable, caring, and safe—what then?

The charming misconceptions and fanciful inventions of a child's mind can delight as well as distress. When he was two, my son Jason enjoyed having a book read to him while we sat on the "dat'n'a." Should we have insisted on the correct word? No way!

For one thing, "rocking chair" simply lacked the intuitive appeal of *dat'n'a*. For another, *dat'n'a* meant more than just rocking chair. Jason had invented the word for back and forth movement—of the chair, yes, but also for the similar movement of a vacuum cleaner and the windshield wipers of our car. Therefore, correcting him would have been wrong, not to mention stupid and unfeeling.

So we sat in the *dat'n'a* and every once in a while Jason would invent a word that became part of our "flammy" [family] vocabulary. Once, we rode on the "pluggett" [public] bus, which wasn't all that "comftaful," but was "very fun." Mark Twain had it right: "The darling mispronunciations of childhood! Dear me, there's no music that can touch it; and how one grieves when it wastes away and dissolves into correctness."

Our children have minds of their own that defy the evidence of their senses. What else explains their charming misconceptions

about the physical world. All chimneys stand straight up from the roof. Nevertheless, children draw them sticking out at an angle.

In time they will draw them correctly not because of what we have taught them but because of what they have learned on their own. Much of it comes despite our teaching! As with chimney drawing, so it is with personality and cognitive development: Much of what children learn—what they care to learn and what sticks for a lifetime—comes from their experimenting more than from our teaching.

When he was three, my son Jason made this smiley-face draw-

ing. He had had countless experiences with humans, none of whom looked like what he had drawn, I assure you. Deep down, he may have known the proper proportionality of human heads and bodies. I expect so, for if suddenly he had confronted a huge-headed human, he might well have been spooked.

Why then did he draw such a big head on a small body? Here's my best guess. While drawing, he was so caught up in a world of feelings and infantile thinking, he naturally lost sight of reality.

Heads have a special significance for carrying faces rich in social signals for learning about people, and family members in particular. Faces carry important information that children need to learn so that they know what they can get away with, how to negotiate for a better deal, how to be sure they are safe and loved, and all sorts of important things like these.

That's why at that tender phase of development, heads must get special attention, and don't even think about pointing out the "error." This surely won't do. One reason it won't do is that, for the child there is no error in following a natural process of social and self-exploration.

So parents, leave it be. Don't interfere. It *should* remain a private affair until it is openly expressed, say in drawings, and then it should be *praised*. "What a beautiful drawing!" And thank you very much for saying so because it *is* a beautiful drawing.

There's another reason it won't do to interfere. Pointing out the "error" won't do any good. For one thing, the child will sense your critical displeasure, and perhaps remember such reactions for a lifetime. For another, the child likely won't know what you are talking about. Good for him.

Of course, disruptive or self-destructive misperceptions or preoccupations will need repeated correction. After all, we parents are responsible for managing the behavior of our naturally reluctant children. We must try to help them learn good conduct despite that reluctance and despite their resistance. So why is it, we wonder, that we encounter so much difficulty getting through to them?

Remember when you were a little kid learning the alphabet? ABCD EFG HI JK *LMNOPeeeeeeee!* QRS TUV W *XYZeeeeeeee!* And so on. Now we need to come clean. How many of us thought that LMNOPeeeeeeee and XYZeeeeeeeeee were words before we learned that they were strings of letters embedded in a much larger string?

No matter that we were singing the alphabet song. If I am right, many of us didn't know what alphabet really meant. When older, how many of us kindergartners pledged allegiance to Richard Stands—remember him? "I pledge allegiance to the flag of the United States of America, and to the Republic for Richard Stands . . . . "

When so much depends on a child's perception and understanding rather than objective facts, how can we even think that we parents have all the power to influence a child's psychological development? The answer is that, in some areas of a child's life, we really don't have all the power.

How else can we explain a string of nightmares that makes no sense to the best parents fretting over their child's fearful imagery and overwhelming anxiety that seems so much at odds with the loving atmosphere that they have always provided?

Yet from the child's perspective, it makes a lot of sense if dreams instinctively explore imaginary worlds that might not be so comfortable, caring, and safe. A child intuitively senses that these worlds might be right below the surface of his family or perhaps right around the corner.

In short, fearful apprehensions can come from an inventive mind capable of fantastical imaginings that might have little to do with the waking world of loving family life, and yet everything to do with the way things might be. That in turn suggests a child's insecurity can trump a parent's kindness.

Again, we see the power that a child's mind and personality have over a parent's best intentions and behavior during early childhood and well beyond. Every so often we even get a wacky reminder of how distant a child's mind can be from a parent's.

A mother was teaching her 3-year-old daughter the Lord's Prayer. For several evenings at bedtime, she repeated it after her mother. One night she said she was ready to solo. The mother listened with pride as she carefully enunciated each word, right up to the end of the prayer. "Lead us not into temptation," she prayed, "but deliver us some e-mail. Amen."

This child had simply not heard or learned what her mother was trying to teach. She couldn't because her mind was bound by more compelling ideas with a similar ring. Another child may simply not understand the meaning of a word, as illustrated by these two charming anecdotes.

A child tells his mother that when he grows up he wants to be a writer and a sidekick. A little confused, the mother finally discovers what her child means by "sidekick."
"It's a detective that looks into the future."
"No," the mother says, "you mean a psychic."
"Yes," the boy says, "a sidekick."

A little girl asks her mother, "Can I go outside and play with the boys?" Her mother replies, "No, you can't play with the boys, they're too rough." The little girl thinks about it for a few moments and asks, "If I can find a smooth one, can I play with him?"

A great chasm exists between what we and our children have in mind—what we parents try to teach and what our children care to learn. This chasm was surely apparent in little Jason's enthusiasm for belting out "Twinkle Twinkle Little Star" with a rousing "up a bug a world so high." Likewise it's evident in an older child's prayer: " . . . and forgive us our trash baskets."

We teach but what do our children learn? Exactly what do they really understand and what do they remember? These are fair questions, given what we are learning about the mind of the child. Consider, for example, some thought-provoking observations reported by psychologist Steven Ceci:

Preschoolers are told a clumsy man named Sam Stone will visit their classroom. Shortly afterward, the man comes in, stays for a few minutes during which he does nothing, then leaves. Four times during the next few months the children are asked leading questions about the man. Remember how the man came into the classroom and broke a toy? Did he do it on purpose or was it an accident?
Initially, the typical child recalls accurately that no toy was broken. After repeated and urgent questioning, however, children start "remembering" things. One child remembers that Sam Stone threw dolls and

books into the air. When another is reminded that it was all just a story, the child insists that it really *did* happen. Another insists that Sam Stone had gone to the corner store to buy chocolate ice cream. Over 70 percent of the children eventually reported imaginary events as real.

Such imaginative qualities of mind reveal yet again how great a difference there can be between what we parents try to teach and what our children are actually learning from others or on their own. Examples of this gulf are all around us in our young children and in their personality and thinking as they grow up into their adolescence and beyond. It's a story of the *inner direction* of child development.

A preschooler is upset with just one piece of cake when his older brother has two. A parent might explain that older children get more and bigger things, and when you get bigger blah blah . . . . Another might say, "Quit whining or you'll get nothing!"

A more creative, kinder approach would be simply to cut the piece into two parts. Often, that's all it takes, and with little frustration or argument. Preschoolers are typically too immature to realize that since each piece is now smaller, together they are no more than the original one. For a preschooler, two is "more" than one, thank you, and that's all that matters. Logic? Evidence? Forget it! Yet how much more pleasant for everyone.

Clearly, a parent's efforts to teach can fail if a child isn't naturally ready to learn. There is a readiness for all things, a certain brain maturity that develops in its own way and in its own time. Failure to learn may therefore be a matter of timing more than laziness or willfulness.

What shall we conclude? When the time is right, teaching can work wonders. That goes without saying. More interesting is this: When the time is right, with the ripening of readiness, *some teaching may not even be necessary.* Learning just seems to happen on its own through observation and personal experience.

Average three-year-olds can copy a circle but not a square. Trying to get them to copy a square is pointless, for a few years later they'll be able to do it without benefit of instruction. Yet five-year-olds who can easily copy a square can't copy a diamond

created merely by rotating that square 45 degrees, as you can see here.

Trying to teach diamond-copying is pointless and for the same good reason. A few years later, those children will succeed on their own, again without benefit of instruction.

As with learning to draw diamonds, so it is with all sorts of things that children must learn, from learning to use the bathroom to learning to read. Before the ripening of readiness, teaching can seem all struggle and frustration. Yet afterward, it can seem natural and satisfying. One father put it this way. "I made strenuous efforts to teach my little Nellie to read from age three onward. Nothing 'took.' Then suddenly, at age six, she started reading. Now seven she reads everything. At the dinner table she reads us the labels on bottles of salad dressing."

So yes, children learn best when they are naturally ready. And this natural readiness is a matter of inner rules that a child must follow. How else can we explain what anthropologist Jared Diamond describes with his own kids.

I have been barraging my sons from early infancy onward with grammatically correct English questions as well as statements. My sons quickly picked up the correct order for statements, but both of them still use the incorrect . . . order for questions, despite hundreds of correct counterexamples that my wife and I model for them every day. Today's samples from Max and Joshua include, 'Where it is?' 'What that letter is?' 'What the handle can do?' 'What you did with it?' It's as if they're not ready to accept the evidence of their ears, because they're still convinced that their [inborn] rules are correct.

Our children's intuitive rules may even defy a parent's vigorous efforts at correction. My favorite example comes from psychologist David McNeill.

A little boy says to his mother, "Nobody don't like me." The mother responds, "No, say: Nobody likes me." The child repeats what he knows, namely, "Nobody don't like me." This sorry interaction goes on eight times. Then the mother says, "No, now listen carefully. Say: Nobody *likes* me." The child thinks for a moment, and says, "Oh! Nobody don't likes me."

We can appreciate the difficulty. The word "likes" is just the opposite of what the child is trying to communicate, which is that people *don't* like him. Clearly, he sticks with what makes sense to him: a better rule. Sticking with his rule means that he won't be able to figure out what his mother is talking about, but so what? Eventually, he'll get it right, yet *on his own terms and in his own good time and without her having to talk about it.* We can only hope that he will come to forgive a mother who seems more concerned about the form of her little boy's complaint rather its substance.

As with learning the rules of language, so it is with learning the rules of social behavior and the rules of life. Yet there are differences. All normal children learn language naturally and effortlessly. When it comes the rules of social behavior and the rules of life, however, our children learn some lessons readily, even gracefully, others clumsily and with great difficulty.

In time some of those difficult lessons will come more easily. Others won't come at all however resolute our efforts or devoted our teaching. The lesson is clear. *What our children learn depends as much on the mental rules they naturally acquire on their own as it does on the social rules we try to impose on them.*

For all of us parents, it's an important lesson to learn. For some of us, it's a comforting lesson; for others it can be truly liberating.

So who's running the show? How much do we really control our children's psychological destiny? How much do our children control their own? And what about *our* psychological destiny? How much were we in control during our own childhood, and how much were our parents?

Chapter 2
Running the Show

Just as all children are subject to parenting, all parents are subject to "childing." So again it seems fair to ask: Are the greatest influences on psychological development mostly what we parents try to make happen or mostly what unfolds naturally from within each child? Who's really running the show? A story shared with me by a good friend suggests an answer.

From day one, each boy exhibited strong individuality. The oldest is still shy and introspective, always concerned with doing the right thing. The middle son is still outgoing, with a take-charge attitude about everything. The youngest is still an observer, going about his business with calm resolve and a matter-of-fact attitude.

When the boys were ten, eight, and six, the family returned to their car in a K-Mart shopping center parking lot only to find the tires flat. It was midnight and deserted, as mom and dad argued over what to do. Embarrassed, the oldest son begged them not to cause a scene. The youngest son got into the back seat of the car and went to sleep. The middle son, at age eight, walked a few steps to Lamar Boulevard and hailed a taxi!

Same family but different personalities. It's like a litter of puppies, one always sleeping, another always crawling, a third always shoving and biting. Differences in our children, so striking from birth, remind us how much their inborn personality traits affect everything we do. They remind us how much our ways of parenting are determined not just by us, but by our children through us.

A child's power over a parent begins with the newborn's appearance, sounds, smell, and touch. All these delicious signals help insure bonding with a parent. They can even transform young men who normally care little for infants. How quickly the sight of his newborn can turn even a macho guy into a mushy dad who is happy, proud and doting too. You know what I mean: sitting there by the bassinet mesmerized by the miracle of new life or maybe creeping in at night to make sure the infant is still breathing. And all that squirming and crying, drooling and pooping? No problem, thank you very much.

In some cases, bonding may be difficult to achieve. Roughly four percent of all children have extremely difficult temperaments. Their sleeping, eating, and energy levels are irregular, unpredictable, and frustrating as are their anxiety and irritability levels as well, all of which can challenge even doting parents.

Temperament researchers Thomas, Chess, and Birch have observed that:

> Such a child will tend to cry loudly when he is hurt whether he has a minor scratch or a deep and painful gash . . . . He may fuss as intensely when he makes a spelling mistake in a minor bit of homework as he may when he makes an error in an extremely important project in which he is engaged. When frustrated, such children may destroy whatever they are working on whether it be a minor construction with tinker toys or a complicated model which has been worked on for several weeks.

Such a difficult child can make some parents increasingly anxious, frustrated, even punitive. It can make others demoralized, distant, or guilt-ridden. Yet here's the key point. Before the birth of their difficult child, these parents were no different from parents whose child turned out normal. Such drastic change illuminates in yet another way a fact of family life. *Our parenting can often be an effect rather than a cause of a child's personality and behavior.*

It may seem we are in control, but only when we forget the powerful influence that our children have on us. Such forgetting may be easy for some, but not for parents with a problem child.

Still, it's easy to imagine poor parenting as the main reason for troubled children. It's easy to say, "No wonder little Billy is so troubled, just look at his parents." Easy, yes, but is it true?

Maybe not, and here's a useful anecdote to help us appreciate why. Nine-year-old Danny is undergoing psychotherapy for anxiety and underachievement at school. During one session, he makes a drawing of a wicked-witch mother eating one of her young while clutching another and trampling a third, while each cries "help."

Should we conclude from this rather gruesome drawing that Danny's mother is a cruel and abusive creature? During doll play,

Danny sticks the mother doll headfirst into the toilet. Is this more evidence that Danny's mother is indeed a horrible person? Granted, she *is* somewhat controlling and overbearing. Yet she is nothing like the demonic creature of the drawing.

Moral of the story: Before we say, "No wonder little Billy or little Danny is so troubled, just look at his parents," I suggest we consider another possibility: "No wonder his parents are so troubled, just look at little Billy or Danny"!

It's a fact of life our children are not mere products of their environment or victims of circumstance. They are not just clay molded by parental potters, for in an important sense *they* are the potter, not we. In countless ways *they* determine what they will be—for better or worse.

By sheer force of their talents and personality, our children create environments that compete with the ones we seek to impose. One way is by actively selecting peers and situations that better suit their needs and dispositions. Another way is by compensating in their own way and on their own. The point is neatly illustrated by an anecdote told by psychologist Nancy Segal.

We studied identical twin girls raised in two very different adoptive English homes. In one home, education was highly valued and the girl—now a grown woman—was given many educational experiences such as easy access to books. Her twin was raised in a very different kind of adoptive family that placed less emphasis on education and learning.

Yet this girl loved to read and learn, so she made heavy use of the local public library. When we brought them both to Minnesota for testing, we found their intellectual levels were quite similar. It was as if one twin utilized the experiences that were easily available to her, while her sister sought them out.

Children not only seek out what they need ready-made in the external world but also create their own world, if only in their mind's eye. Gifted children, for example, compensate for ordinary or even deprived circumstances by force of their intellect and imagination. They borrow books, work through math puzzles, or invent word games. During a moment of boredom, they might make doodles. Here's some "messin' with math," working out proofs done by Jason during an especially boring tenth grade class:

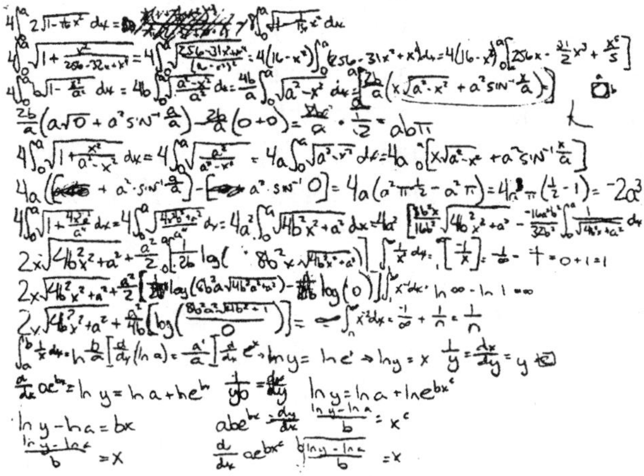

Gifted children offer powerful examples of what all children do in ordinary ways. All start out learning on their own and from examples and instruction. As they mature and move out of the family orbit, they seek out and learn from peers. The talented ones find like-minded peers. The vulnerable find likewise troubled partners. The antisocials find similarly antisocial peers.

Imagine an impulsive boy with strong needs for excitement and adventure. His behavior often clashes with demands for good conduct imposed by his religiously observant parents. While still a child, he occasionally gets into fights or other trouble. Yet his parents' influence limits the full expression of his volatile temperament.

Things change as he gets older and more independent. The high school environment affords him more freedom to exploit various opportunities for rebellion, risk-taking, and drug use. Sure, he is influenced by his environment, *but one largely created by the force and direction of his own personality.*

The sometimes unpredictable ripening of that personality can explain much. It can explain why, despite poor parenting, some children grow up surprisingly secure, inspired, fulfilled and civilized. Yet it can also explain why, despite even good parenting, other children wind up insecure, uninspired, unfulfilled and uncivilized. It can even explain why, regardless of social conditions, a few prove to be monsters who hate, hurt, or even kill people.

Do such facts bring out in sharp relief what is true for ordinary children who become troubled, and for their parents who are desperate for explanations? I think so, which is why focusing on the most troubled children and our reaction to their sometimes dramatic behavior is so instructive.

Too often we seek external reasons, for instance the movies or the Internet, that seem to promote antisocial behavior. We blame gun availability for making terrible crimes more likely. We blame rap music for inspiring antisocial attitudes. And of course, we blame parents for failing to establish rules or monitor behavior. Such blaming makes sense to me; these things do influence children. They do coarsen development, and they do bring out the worst potentials for serious mental illness.

Commenting on the April 1999 killing spree at Columbine High, columnist Jeff Jacoby writes:

More hand holding. More narcissism. More nonjudgmentalism. More worship of self-esteem. More refusal to uphold standards of right and wrong. More of the flight from discipline and character. "Teach them to express their anger?" "Give him a hug?" What the killers of Littleton needed was not more reassurance. Their problem wasn't a failure to express themselves. It was a failure to control themselves, and no wonder. Their lives were filled with adults who never set limits, never imposed rules, never made it clear that certain kinds of behavior would not be tolerated.

Wretched movies, vile lyrics, trashy Web sites, and irresponsible parenting: Sure, any of these may be part of the problem. Yet what about that other part, perhaps most essential, that comes from deep within a highly disturbed child. "These are not normal, healthy teenagers," says psychologist Helen Smith. "They become killers because they are already deeply disturbed individuals who can be sent over the brink by all sorts of innocuous influences."

How do they become so deeply disturbed? Could it be that their emotional problems depend as little on the quality of their rearing as other children's medical diseases depend on the quality of *their* rearing? Well yes, it is a provocative question, but it raises a key point. Blaming parents, a peer group, society, or guns may seem reasonable. There is surely some truth to it, and it is surely satisfying.

Yet any such explanation will remain at best a half-truth if it ignores a basic psychological truth. *Children do a lot to influence their own environment and much of that influence comes from their unique biology.*

Consider a man who, asked what it was like to kill someone, replied:

If you do it in a blind rage, like in a crime of passion, then it's, 'Oops!' If you do it when you're point-blank, stone-cold sober, like I did, if you're able to do it, it's obviously not that damn big of a deal to you. Honest to God, I felt more sympathy for animals I've shot while hunting than I did for Mr. Ward . . . I'm not going to say I'm sorry, because I am not sorry. Whether anyone likes that, it's no concern of mine. Sometimes I wish I could feel bad about it, because maybe I'm supposed to. But I don't.

How can we explain such cruel indifference to human life? Brain damage is one possibility, given that damage to certain parts of the brain can make even happy, productive normal people turn antisocial. Abusive parenting is another possibility, given that an antisocial mentality can be learned in the school of hard knocks.

Yet what about the usual kinds of poor parenting we find in some normal families? Was baby doctor Benjamin Spock correct to say that an antisocial mentality comes from having been unloved during early childhood? If so, then how come some children turn out to be decent adults despite miserable parenting from unloving parents? And why do other children remain awful despite good parenting from decent parents?

Serial killer Carl Panzram always knew he was different from his non-violent relatives.

All of my family are as average human beings are. They are honest and hard-working people. All except myself. I have been a human animal ever since I was born. When I was very young, at five or six years of age, I was a thief and a liar and a mean despicable one at that. The older I got, the meaner I got.

Such depravity is difficult to imagine, yet easy to misunderstand. TV journalist Bill O'Reilly once asked me how a child can become a remorseless murderer. Is the cruel indifference to others that defines the psychopathic mind an effect of parenting or defect of nature? Despite the danger of reducing life to such either-or categories, I nevertheless tried to explain that some children are simply evil—innately evil. For them, no love, no kindness, no moral training will stick.

"Wait a minute," he objected. "How can a newborn who has done nothing bad be evil?" The answer I offered was this: Every psychopathic killer—every Ted Bundy, every "Hillside Strangler" every Hitler—starts out as a cute, innocent-looking babe. The evil is a potential, no less inborn than the potential for diabetes. Call it the dark side of human nature; call it the mark of Cain or original sin.

Call it what we will, each of us carries some potential for evil-doing. An antisocial person carries more than his "fair share," a remorseless psychopath even more. As baby Beethoven's potential was a musical genius and baby Einstein's a scientific genius, baby Hitler's potential was a psychopathic "genius." Unlike normal rebellious antisocial behavior, psychopathic behavior is *not* a matter of poor parenting. The defect is in the brain, not in the parenting.

In some children, this genius for evil shows up early. Such children are loveless creatures who treat other people as mere objects for their own gratification. Unable to feel empathy, they have little concern or remorse about causing suffering.

When older, their callous indifference and gift for the glib reply and the dishonest explanation make them remorseless exploiters of others. Their grossly inflated self-love and sense of entitlement make them effective predators. Being profoundly self-centered, they care not a fig for society's rules. In their mind, only their rules count. They are running the show, not us.

With such a child, even resourceful, well-intentioned parents can accomplish little no matter what they try. One such parent puts it this way:

> He lied constantly. He would steal from our personal belongings to buy nonessential material items, most of which he did not wish or want. He would take our cars for joy rides when we were not aware and he would cover up the activity extremely well. He would bring friends over to the house to have parties without us knowing.
>
> He has always had a need to feel like a special person. Also he has always attempted to buy friends with gifts, parties, etc., so they would look up to him. He associated with children three to four years younger than himself, as they were always impressed with his activities. He could never associate with people his own age, as his behavior lagged his chronological age.
>
> He was suspended from high school for many curfew violations and then he dropped out. We then removed him from the house due to his stealing behavior. He continued to go downhill, getting his own apartment with a false ID so he could have parties with younger high school or junior high girls. He stole an automobile and crashed it and was sentenced to 140 days in jail. He still did not learn. As soon as he got out, he continued the same theft and lying. He was re-sentenced to state jail for four months and is now out. I have not spoken to him since his release three months ago, as I have no idea of his whereabouts.

This child was obviously in control, not his parent. That's clear enough in the frustration and helplessness expressed in the parent's testimony, but even more in his deep sense of loss and demoralization about the failure to have a loving relationship and a positive influence.

> I feel a part of my private life was violated because he lied to me and stole from me after I gave out of sincerity and deep love. I have feelings of being cheated out of not having the fun and enjoyment of molding a son into a successful human being. I feel like I put 110 percent of my energies into making him a successful human being. It never

made any difference. It was as if he was programmed to do what he wanted, and no one else had any control over his behavior . . . .

Such stories of antisocial children illuminate what is true of all children, including ours: their power to resist even our best efforts to shape their personality and behavior. Beyond the social factors of family life and perhaps choice of peers that we mostly can control are deeply inborn forces we mostly can't control. It's just one more reason why a clash of wills is inevitable and, for some of us, even tragic. It's the reason some children are wayward for a time while a few are lost forever, even while their siblings may be no problem at all.

Does any of this mean we parents are off the hook when it comes to responsibility for doing our best? Of course not. Our responsibility for doing our best is always 100 percent. However, our responsibility for how our children turn out is considerably less than 100 percent. It is closer to zero percent for other things, including intelligence, many personality traits, and risk for serious mental illness.

The bottom line: *Our children determine much of their own psychological destiny by remaining true to themselves despite external pressures to be otherwise.*

Chapter 3
Upholding the Self

As their inner potentials ripen, our children's needs become more urgent, their abilities more expressive. These can be frustrated by us, but not happily and not for long. Our children's disposition to revert, sooner or later, to their own ways of behaving remains strong despite what we may try to make happen.

It's as true for children as it is for animals. For example, in return for food, hungry pigs can learn to carry wooden coins to a piggy bank. It's amusing for us yet alien to them, for their piggy "personality" makes them naturally prefer rooting things with their snout rather than carrying them in their mouth. Eventually, powerful inborn preference wins out, so that even hungry pigs will revert to rooting the coins rather than depositing them, though it means a loss of food reward.

We can see in our own children such resistance to instruction and slipping back to inborn ways. All of them are exposed to behaviors modeled by us. All face years of social conditioning with rewards and punishments. Most will learn what they are taught, even things that cut across the grain of personality. Yet in time, they will outgrow or abandon much of what doesn't fit their preferred ways of behaving. They may do so even when such preferences are wasteful, addictive, self-indulgent, or otherwise harmful.

We parents want to give our children every advantage. Yet we go too far when our urging and instruction reflects selfish needs and unreasonable expectations that deny reality. Everything is done for the "good" of the child. The doting parent, all sacrifice and self-denial, has only the best of intentions, but take a closer look at the *quality* of such parenting.

With many such parents, we find an inability to distinguish between what's important to push and what isn't. We find an excessive control of schedules and obsessive commitment to details that reflect insensitivity to a child's need for privacy and free play. We find overbearing response to signs of "success" or "failure" and a continuing push for ever-greater achievement along certain lines. We find parents living through, rather than for, a child.

Take, for example, the overbearing behavior we see at Little League games where agitated parents hurl comments and directives in a desperate effort to correct "mistakes." Such behavior suggests not so much love or respect as a pathological need to turn a child into a pawn or trophy.

A newspaper article describes how a boy with little talent or real interest in baseball is forced to play. He fails, feels inadequate, and wants to quit. According to the article, "one eighth grade student wept in the counselor's office because he did not believe that he could live up to his parents' expectations. The counselor scheduled a meeting with the parents to deliver her professional advice in the bluntest of terms: 'Back off.'"

A parent might object. "We did it for his self-esteem." Yet the nagging question remains. Was it really for his self-esteem or was it for his parents'?

Many parents load up their children with extracurricular classes and lessons to maximize their competitive advantage. Such "hyper-parenting" supposedly boosts academic, athletic, or artistic potentials, yet at what cost? With some children, maybe not much. With others, maybe a lot. With little freedom to be themselves, "over-scheduled" children can become irritable, anxious, even depressed.

Children faced with such parenting can end up resentful and rebellious, whatever benefits they may have had or gratitude and respect they may still feel. "We hold these nuggets of hurt like family heirlooms," says author Deborah Tannen: "bits of conversation in which our parents' disapproval was set like a birthstone in a ring. We clutch them to our hearts, where the edges can continue to scrape . . . . "

We parents can and should impose all sorts of requirements on our children. But does forcing the average child to clean up a room make for a neat person? Not likely. We can and should provide all sorts of opportunities. But does a decade of dance lessons make an average child a graceful dancer? Again, not likely. We can and should provide examples and guidance for good behavior. But, we must ask: How much does any of this change attitudes and how long does any such change last? One thoughtful parent put it this way:

> Amidst our efforts to persuade each other of ideas and attitudes, I've been casting my mind back over my fairly long life, wondering [if] I had ever convinced anyone of anything . . . . I don't think so . . . .
>
> I don't think my conservative father ever convinced me of anything, and my mother, poor dear, who tried various methods to persuade me to assuage society with proper behavior, persuaded me to do quite the opposite.
>
> I had children and though I taught them things, they never learned what I was trying to teach them . . . . I suppose it's like what I call the "hot-stove" syndrome. You can tell children not to touch the hot stove, and they may only learn that you're a nag and, if they touch it when it's cold, a liar to boot, and, they'll eventually touch the hot stove and learn. Maybe when they're forty, they'll think, y'know . . . Dad was right about the stove!

Of course we parents can and should insist on civilized conduct and educational achievement. Still, we must face reality. For some kids, learning good manners and self-discipline may be as challenging as learning to multiply by seven.

We parents can use our influence to secure an advantage for a child, say a slot in a top school or a position in a top corporation. The effort may work wondrously well if a child's talents, focus, zeal, and other qualities of temperament matched the requirements of the situation, in lock-and-key fashion. For example, the father of a brilliant computer programmer just out of college arranges to have his son meet with a venture capitalist. The result is a new company and new opportunities.

Yes, it's wonderful when something like this happens. Yet such efforts aren't likely to turn an ordinary, unambitious child into a high-achieving adult. And the question raised by this fact of social life is key to understanding our influence as parents: Lots of teaching goes on in families, *but what kind of "learning"?* Perhaps much of it is like the learning that happens in high school. How much do we remember about logarithms and polynomials or Julius Caesar and Silas Marner? Exactly what was it that we were actually learning back then?

Professor Robert Hutchins once wrote about a preparatory school whose students had just one more chance to get into an Ivy League college. The instructors were sorely challenged. How should they teach what these students needed to know to pass the exams? The answer was constant drill.

We made sure they could answer every question that had been asked on the College Boards since those examinations were instituted in 1909. As I remember it, our pupils all got into college and all of them flunked out at the end of the first semester. But we had performed our contract. A good deal of [teaching] went on in that school, but very little education.

Likewise, a good deal of teaching goes on in homes, but what kind of "education"? Most children can bend their behavior to a parent's wishes. Yet what use is effort without ability or conformity without conviction if it leads to resentment, failure, or worse. Most children can learn to behave themselves, but not to *be* themselves. The truth of this is neatly illustrated by a story told by psychologist Arthur Jensen about one of America's great composers, perhaps best known for his *West Side Story*.

When Leonard Bernstein was a child, his parents even went so far as to get rid of the piano in their home, because their young son showed such intense devotion to practicing on it they feared he might one day think of becoming a professional musician, a possibility his father extremely wanted to [prevent]. Years later, in Carnegie Hall, after one of Leonard Bernstein's concerts with the New York Philharmonic, a family friend chided Bernstein's father for having tried early on to discourage his famous son's passionate interest in music. The elder Bernstein pleaded, "How was I to know he would become Leonard Bernstein?"

Let's face it. We parents fall short of our goals when we try too hard to make our children much more intelligent, considerate, sociable, assertive, graceful, accomplished, or happier than they are naturally disposed to be. On the other hand, we fail them just as much when we ignore or deny their real talents and temperament.

Personalities are thus like rubber bands, each with different qualities of length, thickness, flexibility, and durability. Social influences, good or bad, are like the stretching that draws the bands out in different directions, in some ways by parents, in other ways by siblings and peers, and eventually by spouses, children, and colleagues.

Right from the start, our children differ in the power of their social instincts to control feelings, thinking, and behavior. These instincts include a need to fit in without being rejected or embarrassed, a need to dominate others, and a need to express their individuality. They also include a sensitivity to social signals regarding rewards—the admiration, acceptance, or submission of others—and punishments—shunning, ridicule—all of which can strengthen or threaten self-esteem.

Social influences from parents and peers can powerfully magnify, warp, or even suppress various aspects of a child's personality. For this reason, personality and social behavior can be quite different at home and at school, often without parents realizing just how different. Even nice kids can wind up doing nasty things, while nasty children can wind up doing nice things, depending on social conditions.

Pulled this way by parents and that way by peers, normal children can be "stretched" quite a bit and for a long time without weakening or snapping. Yet also like rubber bands, they mostly revert to what they are naturally inclined to be. *In the end, what survives to adulthood are those largely inborn qualities that, however stretched by social influences and personal experimenting, nevertheless remain true to themselves.*

This inner direction is touchingly evident in the following anecdote.

At a recent party, schmoozing with one last guest on my way out the door, I suddenly thought, I'm acting exactly like my father! Having spent my youth fighting to forge my own identity, I find, increasingly, that I resemble the very parent against whom I worked so hard to rebel: his social ease, his sense of humor—and, now that I am in my forties, his thinning hair and slight pot belly. Indeed, as I get older, I feel that instead of adding layers, I am shedding skins. In becoming more like my parents, I am becoming more myself. I am surprised but delighted that it all feels so comfortable—not an imprisoning but a homecoming.

* * *

External conditions pull our children while their own experimenting pushes them, often in quite different directions. It's this tug of war between external pull and internal push that reveals most clearly our children's power to remain true to themselves.

It's evident in ordinary children who persist in their ways despite our efforts to shape their behavior in other ways. It's striking in extraordinary children who achieve greatness despite disadvantaged childhood environments.

We are all familiar with famous people from history who started out life poor or neglected. Shakespeare's parents were ordinary folk and none of his five brothers was especially distinguished. Benjamin Franklin was the tenth son of a candle maker. Abraham Lincoln spent his early years in squalid conditions of frontier life. His parents were hillbillies. His father was barely literate. His mother was literate but died when he was nine. Perhaps even more impressive is another such success story.

George Washington Carver experienced appalling misfortunes and deprivations throughout his youth, starting with his birth to slaves during the Civil War. His father died before Carver was born. His mother was abducted while he was still a baby. Brought up by impoverished, barely literate whites, he was denied decent schooling and was forced to take menial jobs. He constantly suffered hunger, bad health, a stammer, and racial discrimination. Despite all this, he managed to get an education and eventually a bachelor's degree in agriculture. Eventually he became a biologist and a celebrated pioneer in the field of agricultural chemistry.

High achievement despite harsh and meager childhood conditions is no better illustrated than by the wonderful story of a singularly extraordinary person. Carl Gauss was born about 200 years ago in a peasant's cottage located in what is now Germany. Little Carl had few educational opportunities during his "formative years." Talk about education disadvantage! What little parental encouragement he did get came from his mother. His father, an uncouth gardener, bricklayer, and canal tender, disapproved mightily of his son's interest in numbers.

That interest had been evident almost from the beginning. According to his relatives, by age two the boy had taught himself to calculate numbers as well as read. One Saturday, when his father was making out the weekly payroll, little Carl, not yet three years old, piped up that his father had gotten a number wrong. He then gave the correct figure, which his father quickly verified.

Carl began formal schooling, such as it was, at age seven. I say "such as it was" because, according to one account, the teacher was "a virile brute, one Büttner, whose idea of teaching the hundred or so boys in his charge was to throw them into such a state of terrified stupidity with his whip that they forgot their names."

One day at school, when Carl was ten, Büttner instructed his students to take up their slates and chalk and add all the numbers from 1 to 100. After completing the task, the children were to stack their slates in the center of the room. Well, about 30 seconds later, Carl walked over to the center of the room, and dropped off his slate.

Büttner was angry. Obviously this insolent child was refusing to do the assignment, for who can add 100 numbers in 30 seconds? Poor little Carl was sent to the headmaster. However, upon collecting the slates, Büttner saw that Carl had written down the correct answer: 5050!

The remarkable boy had realized something neat about that string of numbers. You can pair the 1 with the 100, which adds up to 101. Then you can pair the 2 and 99, which also adds up to 101. You can pair the 3 and 98, which also adds up to 101. Just keep pairing until you use up all 50 possible pairs. The last will be 51 and 50, which, of course, adds to 101. Since each of the 50 pairs adds to 101, you get 50 times 101, or 5050. It's simple enough to see after we are told. Yet how extraordinary for a socially and educationally disadvantaged child to see it so quickly on his own!

Carl's giftedness was frustrated at school by a teacher who was as brutish as he was ignorant. It was frustrated at home by a father whose attitude was that, "Education is a passport to hell." Yet despite such disadvantages during his "formative years," Carl at age nineteen had become the greatest mathematician of all Europe. Some years later, he would become one of the greatest mathematicians and scientific geniuses of all time.

Such amazing stories do more than tell about extraordinary children. They illuminate a deep truth about all children, a truth of such singular importance I will set it off like this:

Much of a child's psychological development is self-determined, not socially programmed. Much of it depends on talent and temperament, not instruction and reinforcement. And much of it resists pressure from external influences that would force it to be other than what it is.

Carl Gauss's story well illustrates this fact of life. It reminds us just how much our kids really are like rubber bands, resisting change imposed by circumstances, but if forced to change, reverting to their normal "shape" when circumstances permit.

This "rubber-band nature," this resiliency of inner self, is most obvious with children who have experienced deprivation or abuse, yet triumph nevertheless. Their awesome stories, the stuff of legend and fable, tell us much about all children.

"I'll tell you what, husband," says the woman, "early tomorrow morning we will take the children out into the forest to where it is the thickest . . . . They will not find the way home again, and we will be rid of them" . . . The two children had also not been able to sleep for hunger, and had heard what their stepmother had said to their father. Gretel wept bitter tears, and said to Hansel, "Now it is all over with us." But Hansel wouldn't give in. "Be quiet, Gretel," he says, "do not distress yourself, I will soon find a way to help us."

These poor wretched children survive their abandonment by force of their inner strengths. Hansel cleverly uses pebbles and crumbs to mark the way back home. Gretel cleverly persuades the witch to get into the oven. In the end, the children return triumphantly with their new-found riches.

Novelist Theodore Dreiser once observed that, "It matters not that the direction of our travel may sometimes be indirect. The needle of our ways of being will yet aim steadfast and unwavering to the pole of an inner compass." Indeed, even despite seemingly impossible odds.

The time-honored fable of Hansel and Gretel is, in my view, more about resilient children than about abusive parents. Lousy parenting or crushing circumstances can provoke aggressive children and scar sensitive children emotionally. Bad environments at home and in the community encourage bad behavior.

Of course, all that's true. Yet most children seem able to muster inner resources to overcome any such scarring. It may take years. It may take a big change in circumstances. But most do, eventually.

A successful business woman once revealed to me harrowing stories of bizarre child abuse that she had to endure for many years. Her crazy mother would beat her for some minor or imaginary infraction, or she would drag her out of school, then scream at her for being home on a school day.

Most impressive, though, was not so much the depth of her trauma as the strength of her character. By that I mean her courage to persist despite crushing experiences and haunting memories. The telling point for me was that a person could wind up doing so well when so much conventional wisdom would have predicted otherwise—that her early experience didn't so much determine her fate as test her character.

During World War II, some children were separated from their mothers and confined to concentration camps. Initially they suffered dreadfully. Yet most eventually turned out fine. Social workers have noted with some surprise how little their personalities seemed affected by their stressful experience.

As one researcher commented: "If orphans who spent their first years in a Nazi concentration camp can become productive adults and if young children made homeless by war can learn adaptive strategies after being adopted by families, then one can question the belief that the majority of insecurely attached one-year-olds are a high risk for later psychological problems."

Such observations reveal how suffering can have a toughening effect on most children. Naturally, some are affected more deeply and differently from others. Their pain might show up in emotional disturbance and social maladjustment. It might go underground, perhaps emerging years later. Yet again, the telling point seems less the emotional scarring than the inner resiliency.

This capacity to bounce back is nowhere more dramatically illustrated than by a unique case, reported in 1972, of two identical twins who had been living in unspeakably horrible conditions.

Their biological mother had died shortly after their birth, so the twins had been placed in a children's home. About a year later, they were retrieved by the newly remarried father.

He was aggressive and physically abusive. His new wife was worse: a classic wicked-witch stepmother, paranoid and abusive. For over five years, she isolated the twins in a small, unheated closet or locked them in a cellar. The twins were severely deprived of decent food, sunlight, fresh air, exercise, toys, and other opportunities to exercise their mental capacities.

When rescued at age seven, the twins had a bruised and battered look. Stunted and suffering from rickets, they were the size of three-year-olds. Their speech was mostly gestures and grunting. They were distrustful, timid, and seemed mentally retarded. After initial hospitalization, they lived in a group home for preschool children. Eventually, they were placed with a family.

Over the next six years, the twins' IQs steadily increased to about 100. This average score is just what we would predict from two facts, given that intelligence is largely hereditary and both biological parents had roughly 100 IQs. Moreover, the children developed into cheerful, inquisitive, well-liked adolescents. According to the report, they excelled in arithmetic, showed creativity and technical talent, and enjoyed reading.

What should we make of the twins' astounding recovery despite unspeakable abuse and neglect during their so-called formative years? None of it denies that children can be scarred emotionally, even for life, by bizarre or beastly conditions. None of it denies that irresponsible parenting is bad or that bad parents are irresponsible.

Rather, it does illustrate how well children can survive all kinds of pressure, even from abusive environments. Sure, they may knuckle under, at least for a time. Yet given half a chance and enough time, most children will revert to their naturally preferred ways.

Perhaps the most spectacular expression of this deep truth is an incredible yet little-known fact. Occasionally, we discover a "brainless" child growing up to be a normal person, with an ambitious personality and a fine intellect. A "brainless" child growing up to be a normal person—what is that all about?

Each day, an infant's brain produces a pint of fluid. If not drained properly, internal pressure can destroy much of the developing brain. The result is hydrocephaly: a child born with "water on the brain."

In the old days, the prospects for such newborns were truly grim. A British mom, facing such prospects, lamented: "I prayed that Sharon would die because I didn't want a cabbage and I vowed she'd never be a cabbage if she lived and I prayed she would die."

Luckily, there was no need for such prayers in Sharon's case. A shunt can be inserted into the brain to drain the fluid. Promptly done, this therapy can minimize some of the mental retardation that results from a damaged brain. In rare instances, something almost magical happens. A child with a shunt can thrive with a normal personality and above average abilities. Sharon, an English girl, was such a child, but an extremely unusual one.

Interviewer: "Do you ever wonder if you are trying to prove anything to yourself?"

Sharon: "I sometimes get the feeling [that] if someone tells me I cannot do something—if they tell me that I'm not good enough to do a thing—I go ahead and just prove them wrong, on purpose."

Interviewer: "Why?"

Sharon: "Because I like to show them what I am capable of."

Sharon's mother: "I always thought she was about average but now I am beginning to consider if she's probably more than average. She passed every exam she took—she didn't fail any . . . In chemistry, she was the only girl to get the GC [general certificate], and in biology, she was one of two girls to get that GC.

These achievements are truly awesome, considering that much brain damage had already occurred while Sharon was still an infant. Her brain was so abnormal it almost seemed to be not there at all. Brain scans revealed a thin disorganized layer of abnormally active tissue surrounding a hollow, fluid-filled cavity, a "watery void" where living brain should be.

Well, the obvious question is: How can a person with such a scrambled brain even be walking around, let alone walking around in a socially normal way? How could a person whose brain may be only 10 percent of normal ever have an IQ higher than 95 percent of the population, and an ability to excel at school?

It boggles the mind that someone with normal instincts, ambitions, feelings, and intelligence could have such a "shuffle brain." Yet the important point for us is not that it can happen. Rather the point is that when it does happen, it reveals in yet another way *the power of a child's inner potential to preserve and defend against even severest challenges from prenatal events and social conditioning.*

In yet another way we see that parents can do only so much to influence the inner forces that drive our children's personal development. Appreciating this fact of social life means two things, one practical, the other moral.

By practical, I mean liberating ourselves from overblown feelings of responsibility and irrational feelings of guilt, in other words, lightening up! By moral, I mean achieving proper humility in the face of nature, in other words, proper humility about what we know—what we *think* we know—about our children and about ourselves. Being smart about such things means accepting in our hearts that we have limited influence and that there are no guarantees for how things will turn out.

I sometimes imagine parenting to be like gardening. We can work the soil, ensure good sunlight, water and fertilize. By keeping up with all those things, our tulips are likely to be the best tulips possible. We can do the same and have the same good results with our irises. Yet our tulips will never be irises and our irises never tulips; neither will they ever be roses, let alone orchids.

Likewise with our children, we can work to make them the best they can be. In this we'll surely have some success, at least while our children are under our control. Yet we cannot make them be what they are not. A tulip child will never be an orchid child. Parents who deny this fact of life are bound to be disappointed. Parents who accept it are bound to be relieved.

Chapter 4
Beyond Childhood

At any age, children go through brief phases when everything seems to change. A compliant child becomes rebellious, a confident child becomes anxious. Children also go through more lasting stages. A preschooler is a different kind of creature from a fourth grader. Likewise, an adolescent is a different kind of creature from a ten-year-old. Journalist Leonard Pitts describes it this way.

> Anyone who has been a parent for any appreciable time can tell you, a child inevitably reaches an age where there's absolutely nothing you can do that he will not find mortally embarrassing . . . . Any parent who's honest, though, will admit that it hurts a little to be, well . . . rejected. Wasn't it just yesterday that this child considered me the fount of all things wise and good? How is it that now he doesn't want anyone to know he came from me?

A parent's relationship with an adolescent is threatened by many things. An obvious one is the influence of peers and popular culture. As one parent said, "I can teach my children the old values all I want, but what if they see that nothing bad comes from doing otherwise? In that case I don't see much chance that they will have the same manners and values as I do, and even less chance that they will pass those values on to their children."

Another threat to a parent's influence is the influence of brain development, especially in the front part that is still immature during adolescence. Connections in brain networks are still developing, which means the capacity for judgment, planning, and self-restraint is still years away. As brain researcher Daniel Weinberg neatly put it:

This is why it is important for adults to help children make plans and set rules, and why institutions are created to impose limits on behavior that children are incapable of limiting. Parents provide their children with a lend-lease prefrontal cortex during all those years that it takes to grow one, particularly when the inner urges for impulsive action intensify.

Starting with puberty, the immature brain undergoes major changes. Some parts can increase in connections up to 80 percent. Others can decrease 50 percent. All this can alter an adolescent's personality, sometimes even without stressful social conditions.

The alteration can involve an intense competition between parts of a personality, the "good" and the "bad." It's why our adolescents can be so maddeningly inconsistent, shifting from sharing to being secretive, from loving to hating, from being responsible one moment to irresponsible, even self-destructive, the next.

A conflict between the "good" and "bad" aspects of their inner workings can drive some children to destruction. If strong enough, the clash of Jekyll-Hyde forces within can defy even the best efforts of frustrated parents.

Sure, it's easy to love little kids when they seem so cute, happy, and manageable. It's quite another matter to love the willful child or the wayward adolescent who defies our teaching or worse, who departs from the family orbit, sometimes suddenly and with surprising ferocity. As one parent observed, "I think it's the overnight rebel who is often our undoing because we have no time to adapt."

Indeed, how can a parent adapt when a deep feeling of loss competes with a strong sense of good riddance! Two elderly women sitting on a park bench are complaining about their kids.

One asks: "Tell me, if you had the chance, would you have children again?" "Yes," replies the other, *"but not those two!"*

The clash of wills can sometimes be hard to bear. A child feels the crush of resentment, a parent the sting of ingratitude. Novelist Samuel Butler put it this way: "Imagine what it must be to have [a child], who is of an entirely different temperament and disposition to your own . . . [a child] who will not love you though you have [tried so hard] in a thousand ways to provide for [his] comfort and well-being—who will forget all your self-sacrifice . . . .

The effects of such ingratitude and wayward behavior can be devastating. For illustration, consider an adolescent girl who rejected her parents while embracing a self-destructive relationship with her psychopath boyfriend. Here's what happened, first in the mother's words, then in the words of her daughter.

[Mother] Carol went off to 9th grade with great expectations. She was one of the top students in her class, a good athlete, popular with her classmates and very naive. Drugs were a complete turnoff to her and she was not into sex, drinking or breaking the rules. We thought we had it made.

Well, 9th grade started and a few weeks into school Carol started talking about this boy she had met. I didn't think he sounded too good, but she assured us he was sooo nice and please give him a chance. As it turned out, the first time we let Carol meet him at the park, she came home late. I had to go looking for her twice and always got the same, "I am so sorry." This was the beginning of the two-year nightmare.

From that day on, we slowly began to lose Carol to John. From coming home late, going places she wasn't supposed to go, skipping school, his control grew and grew. My husband and I tried every conceivable way to try to break her free from this "bad seed," but to no avail. We just knew that Carol was headed for disaster with this guy and we had no control. Carol was the best thing that happened to him, and he was the worst thing that happened to her. He was so smooth, and later on we found out that this was a pattern with him. Prey on young innocent girls and corrupt them. His goal was to destroy everything that was good in her life, all under the guise of "love."

After about six weeks Carol dropped all of her honors classes, quit her sports, quit most of her friends, and quit us. She had time only for

John. She was still going to school and living at home. But the fighting was horrible and in her eyes it was all our fault. She was totally brainwashed by this piece of shit.

Carol started stealing money from us and sneaking out at night. Soon she was on all kinds of drugs, having unprotected sex and God knows what else. Her new friends, John's friends, were dropouts and druggies.

Nine months had gone by and we were on our vacation. Carol was very sick and I thought she had the flu. Well, she was pregnant. She and I discussed the situation and she decided to have an abortion. A decision we definitely supported. Between all the drugs and being only 15 years old, I was not about to raise the spawn of a real psychopath.

Our family had been suffering terribly. I was beginning to "hate" Carol, and her sister still complains about those years that Carol "ruined" her life. John continued to be a thorn in our side. My husband and I sat up one night and decided that the only way we could get John out of Carol's life was to kill him. We had a discussion as to which one of us should do the deed. Whose loss would affect the family the least. Never in a million years did we ever think that we were capable of such thoughts.

One morning Carol came home after being gone all night to find her clothes in garbage bags on the front lawn. I had kicked her out and she couldn't believe it. She totally freaked out and said that she couldn't live with John and that she didn't want to leave us. When he sensed this, he began attacking us and that pushed Carol away from him and back to us.

When Carol began taking her Zoloft regularly and started feeling better, she became stronger. She began concentrating on school again, joined the soccer team, and started spending more time with us. Eventually she left John, but, at what cost? It took me years to accept the "new" Carol. My husband still has problems. I don't think he will ever get over the experience. He dearly loves Carol but John took his little girl away and a grown woman came back in her place. Carol sacrificed a great deal. She regrets having lost her youth but realizes there is nothing she can do about it.

[Daughter] . . . I consider my experience with John to have been a "brainwashing" experience. I met him when I was very young and naive, and I gave up my entire life for him. He became so dependent on me that it made it practically impossible to get away. In any situation where I chose to be with my family, John went absolutely ballistic because he knew that he could not shield me from the truth that my parents wanted so badly for me to believe . . . .

Next thing you know, I'm running away from home and totally turning on my family as if they were my enemies. My friends' houses were simply an escape for me to see John. In no time, he had gained control over me, my family, and whatever else he wanted, and without me ever knowing what he was doing. I thought it was out of his love for me, and I even wanted to marry the asshole. I was engaged to him at 14, and ready to give up everything to be with him.

Finally, I woke up. I realized that my life could be so much simpler if I would just get rid of him, and I did. The realization that John was scum and the courage to tell him that I didn't want to be with him anymore came from within me, no one else. I just did it one day because I was *truly* fed up in my heart. It took all of that pain and agony for me to realize it, but finally the miracle happened. I opened my eyes and said "I've had ENOUGH!"

[Mother] I am no longer the judgmental person I used to be and am much more accepting. Not only that, I no longer feel so guilty about what I might have done wrong to make all this happen. Basically my new philosophy is that a lot of things happen outside your control, so deal with it as best you can, learn from it as much as you can, and move on.

The changes described by Carol and her mother illustrate how social conditions outside a parent's control can stir up the awesome potentials of an adolescent. To me, it's a little like what happens to the tadpoles of the pudgy spadefoot toad. Normally, these little guys are serene, sociable creatures. You might even say they are really "good kids." But when food and water become scarce, the stress can trigger dramatic change. As one observer put it, some of them turn mean and cannibalistic, with big heads and giant mouths filled with oversized teeth!

All this will seem familiar to parents struggling with a newly rebellious, disagreeable adolescent. How, they wonder, could such a lovely tadpole have become such an alien toad! The answer: inborn vulnerability, perhaps long hidden until roused during puberty by hormonal changes that help make even normal social conditions stressful. We have seen how this transforming mix can lead to unhappy, even destructive, consequences that in many cases could not have been foreseen.

Changes in the immature brain during puberty can explain more ordinary psychological developments. For instance, it can explain why an adolescent becomes impossibly self-conscious and self-critical or gives over to boorish behavior, faddish dress, and thuggish friends. Writer Shannon Brownlee notes:

> If there is one thing that drives parents nuts about their teenagers, it's moodiness. "It's hot and cold, nasty and nice," says Vicki Sasso, 34, the mother of 13-year-old Angelo . . . . "One minute loving me, one minute hating me." Don't blame Angelo; blame the parts of his brain that process emotions and make decisions. And just as a teenager is all legs one day and all nose and ears the next, different regions of his brain are developing on different timetables.

Perhaps changes in the brain can even explain this notation in a medical chart: "Patient has two teenage children, but no other abnormalities." In short, biological changes can explain why adolescence can seem like temporary insanity! How strange for the poor frustrated parent of one such adolescent who wonders, where did *that* child come from?

Not until about age 20 will innate changes in the brain be mostly complete. This could explain why most adolescents, having passed through the "puberty pipeline," eventually settle down and turn out fine. It's why they are likely to experience what we might call the "Mark Twain insight." When he was 14, the writer says, "my father was so ignorant that I could hardly stand to have him around. But when I got to be 21, I was astonished at how much the old man had learned."

Yes, most adolescents turn out fine, but some do not. In either case, we confront the limits of our influence as parents. With troubled adolescents exhibiting any of three patterns of change, this fact of family life is merely more evident.

• *A good child becomes wayward for a time.* Such children, now adolescent, have suddenly turned rebellious, sexually promiscuous, drug abusive, and even antisocial. They put themselves and their parents through hell. Eventually though, they come to their senses and return to the fold. Their prospects are mostly good. (Recall the story of Carol.)

• *A bad child gets even worse.* Such children—from an early age antisocial, rebellious, or vulnerable—are headed for a lifetime of difficulties. Their prospects are mostly poor. (See the story of Jack on page 85.)

• *A good child becomes habitually antisocial, even criminal.* The likely cause is a genetic factor that ripens during puberty and flourishes thereafter. Over time their problem gets worse despite even heroic parenting and professional help. Their prospects are mostly poor.

This third pattern is touchingly illustrated by a demoralized father's heart-felt story about his good child hopelessly devastated by drug addiction:

In all major respects, Tracy seemed a happy and well-adjusted child. She was bright, funny, and affectionate. She had many friends and enjoyed all manner of school and extracurricular activities. She often expressed love and delighted in doing nice things for people, especially her brother and her parents. She had a directness and honesty that most people found refreshing. She often had an air of mischief but with no trace of mean spiritedness. She had an innate sense of right and wrong, expressing anger only when she felt an injustice had been done. She loved animals. She was endlessly compassionate about people who were down on their luck. She laughed easily and often. She was just a great kid.

For my wife and me, and for anyone who knew her as a child, the change in Tracy's personality and behavior beginning at age 14 was genuinely shocking. That's when she began abusing drugs. By age 15 she was already displaying many of the warning signs of addiction. Several times a week, she would sneak out of the house at night. Her grades dropped from straight As to Ds and Fs. She stopped socializing with friends she had grown up with. She began to hang out with a new crowd of people who were no longer in school and who sported tattoos, body piercing, multicolored hair, and sullen demeanors.

In December 1995 she was detained by the police for breaking and entering. The following July, she was arrested for credit card theft, a state jail felony. Later that year, she was charged with a shoplifting misdemeanor and paid a small fine.

After obtaining her driver's license, she was declared at-fault in a series of car accidents, three of which caused major property damage. Luckily, she was never injured. She has admitted that drugs and alcohol were factors in all of these accidents. During this past year, she has been arrested twice for public intoxication and three times for alcohol-related driving offenses.

Not long after that, my wife and I found hypodermic needles and other IV drug paraphernalia in her room. For the first time, we had her tested, and she registered positive for opiates. She then admitted that she had been using heroin almost daily for a long time. She also said that she had "kicked the habit" several days earlier with the help of her older brother Ritchie who, she told us, is also a heroin addict. (We discovered that Ritchie was then undergoing outpatient detoxification under the care of a physician who specializes in treating heroin addicts.)

When she is using drugs, Tracy is generally ill-tempered, resentful, dishonest, selfish, manipulative, spiteful, and, in some cases, violent. Most of her friends and acquaintances have lost patience with her and have withdrawn their emotional and financial support. She is simply out of control. As long as she continues to use alcohol or drugs, my wife and I have decided Tracy cannot live at home or receive any financial support from us. The decision to tell her this was painful for us, but we felt we had to do it . . . .

As a family, we had been very close. My wife and I have been married for 25 years and have a warm, loving, respectful relationship. We always treated our kids with love and affection, and we spent a great deal of time with them. We gave our children ample encouragement without setting unreasonably high standards. We usually had a lot of fun when we were together since all of us shared a similar sense of humor and enjoyed many of the same activities.

I always believed, perhaps too smugly, that we were a model family, something like in "Leave it to Beaver." The events of the last four or five years have pretty much eliminated that idea. They have forced me to understand how little control my wife and I have over our children.

Puberty had transformed a sunny disposition into something dark and sinister. The daughter grew increasingly aggressive, truant, and sexually promiscuous. Eventually she tried to burn down her parents' house because, she said, they refused to buy her a car. In this case as with countless others, we cannot reasonably blame parents for such monstrous transformations of personality and behavior, not when the fault may be inborn changes in brain activity.

With all such troubled children we can clearly see yet again what is true for all of us, yet still overlooked by most of us and therefore bears repeating. Our full responsibility for how we raise our children is one thing. Our limited responsibility for how they turn out is quite another.

Failure to appreciate the difference is a major reason why some parents, challenged by difficult children, have had to endure much unnecessary confusion and grief. It's why one specialist can say, "Parents are challenged at every level in their often stormy relationship with such problem children. Despite looking into every new fad and trying every possible intervention and support group, they may still wind up feeling like failures." It's why a typical complaint is that, "We parents really don't have anyone who understands what we are having to deal with and how much we feel personally responsible."

The situation of such parents differs from the norm merely by degree, for we are all more or less in the same boat. We all have our hopes and dreams for our children. Yet we can do only so much with any child, and with some children, rather little. Perhaps accepting this fact of family life can afford some measure of comfort at those times we are most conscious of that nagging question: Whose child is this anyway?

How poignant then are the words of Ecclesiastes. "I looked on all the works that my hands had wrought, and on the labor that I had laboured to do: and behold, all was vanity and vexation of spirit, and there was no profit under the sun."

PART 2

HOPES AND DREAMS
Parents' Impact on Children

Chapter 5

Heart of Darkness

Our essential job must be to protect our children not just from physical dangers or even from others, but from themselves. This means making every effort to civilize barbarous instincts that could drive them to destruction.

We recognize such instincts in the cruel, selfish, destructive behaviors that appear right from early childhood. In birthday parties for three or four-year-old boys, for example, we can see delightful behavior that is no doubt cute, charming, and amusing. Yet we can also see behavior that is both selfish ("It's mine!") and mean spirited ("I hate you!"), aggressive and greedy ("Gimme that!"). We can even see behavior that seems downright delusional ("I didn't do it . . . Anyway he made me do it!").

We can readily see these nasty dispositions in any setting—the family, the school yard, and in psychological studies. One of the most dramatic ones involving boys attending summer camp was reported in the late 1940s. Good friends were forcibly split up into two groups called Bull Dogs and Red Devils.

This interference with friendships drove the frustrated boys to protest vigorously. Yet soon enough, those former friends now in opposing groups—two gangs, really—gradually shed their old loyalties and became mortal enemies. Eventually, violent conflicts among the children forced the investigators to call off the study lest someone got seriously injured or even killed!

A similar story is told by novelist William Golding. In his visionary classic *Lord of the Flies*, English schoolboys stranded on an island revert to barbaric outrages against former friends. Stripped of the civilizing influence of community and family, even "good" boys brought up by good parents had become nasty creatures who preyed on former friends.

The awful truth of Golding's insight became all too apparent during the filming of the book's movie adaptation. It was then that director Peter Brook made a shocking discovery. Some of his child actors were so caught up in the story they had become the predatory, murderous creatures they had been portraying!

Golding was dramatizing a fact of social life. The civilizing influence of even good parenting is a rather fragile thing requiring constant vigilance. There's always that potential for mayhem lurking just below the surface, stronger in some children, weaker in others.

We may know all this intuitively, yet still assume that with even minimally decent parenting, older, more civilized children know better and therefore will behave better. We may also assume that our children will be as civilized elsewhere as they are at home. The facts suggest otherwise. Columnist Joan Vinnochi describes a night of laser tag played by young adolescent boys. They had been dropped off at midnight by their parents and mostly left to themselves till 6:00 A.M.

> As the night wore on, the activity took on an eerie malevolence . . . . The scary part was not what the boys were wearing or even what they were doing, but the look on most of their faces as they did it. They weren't smiling or laughing; they were nervous and jittery. They didn't look as if they were pretending or fantasizing. They seemed deadly serious about tracking down and killing off one another . . . . Finally, one remained—the winner. Wearing a triumphant look, but still no smile, he raised his hands in victory. The watching boys cheered.

When circumstances permit, "nice" older children can revert to vicious bullying, scapegoating, back stabbing, ridiculing, shunning, or ostracizing. Special targets are children who display any physical or psychological difference from the norm, especially in the form of obnoxious or otherwise provocative traits.

Occasionally it can have tragic consequences, for example when taunting, belittling, isolating, or bullying enflames a volatile mix of delusion, rage, and violence.

A notorious example involved the killing spree committed on April 20, 1999, by two adolescents who stormed into Columbine High School killing 12 classmates, their teacher, and finally themselves. A high school student commented: "To shoot all those people? Make bombs? You have to be sick, and the question they should be asking isn't what [video] games they play. How come all these high paid administrators, parents, teachers and so-called professional people—how come none of them noticed how wacked they were?" Wacked out indeed, for according to columnist Dave Cullen:

> The attack launched April 20 was planned as a suicide mission, driven by indiscriminate hate, and intended to wipe out most of their suburban school. Their hatred was boundless, often ludicrous. In his so-called diary . . . Harris raged against everyone from slow drivers in the fast lane to the Warner Brothers network. And his celebrated "hit list" . . . included targets as bizarre as Tiger Woods. His diary opens with the telling phrase: "I hate the fucking world."
>
> They were equal-opportunity haters, railing against minorities and whites, praising Hitler's "final solution"—and then ranting against racism. Their scribblings also reveal standard teenage concerns: The same writings where Harris described his plans to destroy his school April 20 found him obsessing about finding a date for the prom, held three days earlier.

Adverse social conditions are especially hard on vulnerable teens. One noted that junior high school girls "are so cruel and horrible that no one can stand them." Cruel behavior need not be either spontaneous or informal. It can be a formal or ritual part of group initiation. Many high school students who join clubs, teams, or other groups must endure humiliating or dangerous forms of hazing. These can take the form of being cursed at or isolated, for instance, or being forced to serve an older member.

Dangerous hazing can involve the abusive use of alcohol or even illegal drugs. It can involve crank calls, stealing, cheating, vandalizing property, and engaging in other criminal activity. The survey's findings prompted an observer to note that initiation rites can turn into a kind of Lord-of-the-Flies scenario.

The heart of darkness is more than the instinct for cruel and aggressive behavior. It's the instinct for devious behaviors. Because these come naturally and often work so well, we may be taken by surprise. A parent offers this example of how slick and subtle such dishonesty can be in even a normal child:

My son Sam would never tell an outright lie, but he is willing to tell less than the whole truth. His second grade teacher put his name on the chalkboard if he failed to follow the rules. My husband and I asked him every day after school, "Did you get your name on the board?" and he would answer truthfully. When he was in the third grade, we asked the same question, and the answer was always "No." We were thrilled that his conduct was so exemplary.

Then we learned from his teacher that she had changed the policy; names were no longer written on the chalkboard but on index cards. We went home from parent-teacher conferences to confront our son. "Sam, you lied to us. You told us you were good." Sam replied earnestly, "No, I did not lie to you. You asked me if I got my name on the board, and the answer was always 'no.'"

My husband looked at me and sighed. "Dear," he said, "we are raising a president!"

Responsible parents continually work to civilize naturally reluctant children. After all, we know they are simply too needy, naive, and self-centered to appreciate many things adults take for granted, for instance, the Golden Rule. With our youngest we earnestly ask, "How would you like it if your brother hit *you*?" We ask even if we suspect the child really doesn't understand the principle.

No matter, our youngest must learn to do the right thing even before they learn—even if they never learn—why doing the right thing is the right thing to do. We must therefore try to get our children to learn that they can't always have what they want when they want it, and that rewards depend on good conduct.

If we are lucky, our children will eventually learn a difficult moral lesson: that high intelligence without good character isn't good enough, nor is honesty without courage. They will learn to be considerate despite themselves, to appreciate the limits of their entitlements, and to understand that they have social responsibilities as members of a family and the larger community. Finally, they will come to know that selfishness or getting by is not acceptable and that "good enough" is simply not good enough.

All this means letting them know two important things: first, that they have it in them to do well (unless, alas, all signs say they don't) and second, that when they need us, we will be there for them. These two things are captured in the following snip from a father's poem written on the occasion of his son's thirteenth birthday.

> Recall the guy who leaped from Brooklyn Bridge,
> Who, as he fell, looked back to where he'd stood
> And, struck with philosophic irony,
> Achieved this insight, that: "So far so good."
>
> "So far, so good" is fine, but not enough.
> Just getting by will surely not suffice.
> When sorely pressed and things get really tough,
> We tap our wisdom for the right device.
>
> Yours will come, I have no doubt of that,
> From sources now you barely understand.
> And as you take your turn at bat
> Your mom and dad can lend a helping hand.

Parenting is no easy job, and it will surely fail with some. Still we must make the effort to help children learn to contain their dark side. Yet some parents have trouble setting limits and saying no. The discomfort of frustration, the fear of losing love, the pleasure of indulgence: Any of these can make a parent give in to insistent badgering.

The unintended consequences of such appeasement, however, are children with a heightened sense of entitlement and a dimin-

63

ished sense of responsibility. Such children demand privileges but avoid obligations, blame circumstances rather than criticize themselves.

Children are naturally inclined to exploit their environment, for instance, by avoiding responsibilities or extracting bribes for good behavior. Parents who give in are at risk of becoming hostages to selfish, greedy kids. Taking the easy way out yields little in the way of genuine love, admiration, or good conduct.

Journalists have sounded the alarm. One wryly notes: "More American parents are unleashing uninstructed savages onto society—young people who lack the advantages of having been raised by wolves."Another puts it this way. Too many parents would rather "whine and wheedle, lie and litigate, [in an effort] to replace the C that little Susie honestly earned with an A she did not."

With severely "spoiled" children, respect for people and property can be a major casualty. A recent poll of 8,600 teens suggests a shockingly high prevalence of immoral attitudes or antisocial behavior. Many teens admit that during the prior 12 months they have cheated (70%), lied to parents (92%), stolen something from a store (40%), and, in the case of males, gone to class drunk (17%). Many also admitted they had physically assaulted another person (68%) and knew how to get a gun (47%).

Insofar as we parents normally make a difference for the better, surely it must be in helping a child deal with poor judgment and destructive impulses. Most essential are rules and restrictions usually taught by instruction and example.

All children need to learn how to behave in a civilized manner—even better, in a considerate and courteous manner. Whatever the techniques we use, our children will wind up learning many things best in their own way and in their own time. So the challenge for us parents is how to balance our demands and our children's capabilities. Excessive demands for conformity and self-control or for being more competitive and sociable may seem perfectly justified. Yet we pay a price when even reasonable demands cut deeply against the grain of a child's personality.

Still, we have to try, and hope for the best. Love mixed with discipline seems to be the key. Some techniques may seem harsh, for instance, occasionally allowing children to experience the consequences of screwing up. Yet this can also teach discipline and morality, and much better than fine words or protective bailouts ever could. Some things are best left to a child to learn through experience, says psychologist Stanton Samenow.

Fearing that their children will fail, parents sometimes step in too quickly to do for their offspring what they could eventually accomplish for themselves. Or they might rush in to bail a child out of a jam that he created by his own irresponsible behavior. Such attempts by parents to accommodate their children are ill-advised, because they can deprive a child of the opportunity to learn something worthwhile. A child might procrastinate or ignore a task if he thinks he can count on a parent to step in and resolve a problem for him. Or if he is rescued and spared some unpalatable consequence, he may expect that someone will always be available to bail him out.

Other techniques may seem cruel, yet may prove to be just the measures needed, like a firm slap on the rear when all else fails. Author Jerry Pournelle observed that:

Having raised four boys to manhood without losing any to the police, drugs, or madness, and without having drugged any of them, I can tell you this. Boys need a heck of a lot of imposed discipline so that they can learn self-discipline . . . . When I was young we were seldom beaten, whipped or otherwise struck. But we were somewhat afraid of it, and more, we could use that fear with our peers. "I'd love to do that with you but my folks would beat me to a pulp." Of course they wouldn't beat me to a pulp, but by putting forth something we all legitimately feared, we had a good reason not to put bags of burning dog-turds on the neighbor's front porch and do other things that we thought would be a very good thing to do except that the consequences would be severe . . . .

Particularly challenging are bratty, grumpy, anxious, willful, impulsive, defiant, or aggressive children. Yet heroic efforts to manage their troublesome behavior can sometimes teach a measure of self-discipline and social competence. Yet with some children, moral training fails to sink in. Even if it does sink in, it doesn't much control pressing needs or raging reactions. Either way, we have a formula for disaster. As TV journalist Bill O'Reilly rightly notes:

Some people are born self-destructive. There's nothing anyone can do about it. Some children will fail, no matter what, just as some will succeed when the circumstances of home life are against them . . . . The son of one of the finest guys I know is a heroin addict. This selfish young jerk abandoned his own daughter, so his father is helping to raise her. The dad, who feels terrible about the whole situation, sometimes blames himself for his son's weakness and cruelty. No one else does. We all know that it is entirely the son's fault. He was unreachable.

Most of our children normally do manage to become reasonably social and civilized in their behavior. Even if they go a little crazy for a while, most of them do eventually return to their senses and to those unique qualities of personality, intelligence, and character that mark them as individuals for a lifetime.

All these observations about the inner workings of a child's human nature suggest two essential "Rules of Good Parenting." Rule 1 summarizes what we've been saying: that good parenting means *helping children become civilized and socially responsible.* It's what we might call the fine art of managing behavior to protect children not just from physical or social harm, but from themselves. This means managing behavior in the home but where possible, managing a child's choice of peers who influence a child's behavior for better or worse.

With that fine art firmly applied, our children have their best chance to develop a sense of responsibility for their behavior and a firmer sense of who they are and what they stand for. Of course there are no guarantees that our best efforts will work as well as we would like. But one thing is as certain as death and taxes: Without trying, without vigorously confronting the dark forces of human nature, our children will turn out far more selfish, immature, and antisocial than they would otherwise have been.

Rule 2 says *good parenting means respecting children, not just loving them.* Respect means dealing intelligently and humanely with our children's needs to preserve and express their individuality. This means, for instance, considering their opinion on various things from family matters to current events.

It also means appreciating that, along with their family obligations, they have needs for privacy and exclusivity, that is, for a time and place of their own and for defending what belongs to them as opposed to what belongs to each of the other siblings or what all the children share in common.

Respect means likewise dealing intelligently and humanely with our children's deepest concerns and worries, including:

• *challenging situations* involving, for instance, a new baby, sibling rivalry, parental conflict, parental drug use, or peer pressure to get involved with drugs and, often much too early, sexual activity, which is especially anxiety-provoking and potentially traumatizing for girls;

• *emotional stress* involving anxiety, envy, anger, despair;

• *self-confidence,* especially doubts about competition with siblings, fitting in socially, and performing academically, especially during crises involving failure;

• *interpersonal questions* especially involving dating, going steady, and sexual commitment, about which much may be secret if not communicated with much reluctance;

• *personality traits and personality changes* involving secretiveness about their introversion, shyness, sensitivity, or emotional turmoil, even emotional withdrawal, anxiety, hostility, and apparent inability to understand, let alone appreciate, how irrational or even destructive their behavior can be;

67

- *moral questions* involving honesty, loyalty, obligation, entitlement, justice, honor, especially when situations stimulate the worst of human nature to urge the very opposite: dishonesty, disloyalty, and dishonor through self-indulgent, self-centered behavior that goes well beyond what society deems acceptable; and finally

- *ultimate questions* about life, death, religion, and God.

Some observers have noted that puberty can erupt in crisis and impasse, making it harder to apply the rules successfully. Relatively high rates of delinquency, school dropout, teen-age suicide, drug addiction, and runaways are only the most dramatic symptoms of this problem. "Even 'normal' adolescence is full of anxiety and, far from opening the doors to a more whole and complicated self, it tends to benumb us morally and intellectually."

The problem, they note, is that adolescents are treated by parents as if they were large children. "And under these circumstances, the adult forces which are forming in them lash out and wreck terrible vengeance." Wise parents recognize the change. They appreciate the evolution of their child into adult and show respect for their developing needs for recognition as adults. In many ways they *are* adult, though without appreciating that they are not fully formed adults and therefore lack the full range of adult privileges and responsibilities.

Wise parents understand that adolescent children may at times seem delusional, even "crazy." They may even suspect some brain abnormality! No wonder some parents really do think of themselves as an external frontal lobe for their adolescents! Nevertheless, they can take comfort in knowing that, however secretive or resentful they may be, such children do hear and hold in their memory what parents share in their typically urgent, yet loving, non-accusatory manner.

Deep down, their children likewise find comfort in knowing that their parents can be trusted and that they really do care about what they think and what they feel. It's the kind of realization that can affect in a positive way lifetime thoughts and feelings about a parent and about family relationships. Good illustrations of such "coming around" to "see the light" are stories such as Albert's (p. 148) and Carol's (p. 49).

Respect for children also means continuing to encourage their best instincts and evident talents and zeal, say for art, music, science, or sport. Parents do this even when their child's interests turn out different from what the parent would have preferred. Psychologist David Lykken tells of a professor whose son's only interest was cars and engines. "That father might have pushed and prodded his son through college into some unfulfilling white-collar career. Wisely, he let his son study auto mechanics and helped him to establish his own garage, which the university faculty patronized enthusiastically because the young man did such good work."

Wise parents know it may take a variety of experiences before some possible hidden ability or talent is triggered. They also know that their efforts can be ruined by distractions from peers and from their children's own newly developing sexual impulses and need for autonomy and social acceptance. Finally, they know not to push children beyond their abilities and to ease off when they recognize that a talent or passionate commitment to the hard work of developing a talent just isn't there.

In all of this, good parenting at home is like good teaching at school. Psychologists Camilla Benbow and Julian Stanley's views on the educational needs of gifted children readily apply to our children.

We need to provide all children with an equal opportunity to learn and develop to their full potential. This is consistent with the true meaning of education. The Latin root of the word education is *e-ducare*, which literally means to lead forth or to bring out something that is potentially present.

In this view, each of our children has distinct needs for different responses from us, different approaches to curb their worst impulses while promoting their best. It is no easy matter balancing what we do firmly but fairly for all our children with what we do with each differently. Still, good parenting means trying one's best, regardless of how much our child understands and regardless of how much of what we try to accomplish sticks for the long run.

No doubt, normal parenting styles, the positive and the negative, affect children's behavior and therefore the quality of family life. And no doubt they matter to what children learn and therefore to lifelong feelings about their parents. Perhaps a parent and child will end up good friends who enjoy each other's company. Perhaps they might become mere formal allies with mixed feelings toward each other. Alas, they might wind up as emotional foes who can barely stand each other.

For this reason, we need to appreciate another aspect of Rule 2, which says *children are not mini-replicas of their parents.* Our children may feel pressure to conform to our hopes and dreams; they may even identify with these, at least for a while. Yet eventually, they have little choice but to follow their own psychological paths, despite what we parents try to make them do.

Perhaps most difficult of all, we parents must learn when it is time to let go, even when our emotions say hang on. Over the years, our children naturally tend to move away from us, psychologically and physically. Most do so despite their love and loyalty. Informed parents understand this biological fact of social life. Wise parents embrace it or at least resign themselves to it. They know that *everything they do, if truly in a child's interest, should foster natural competencies for independent and autonomous growth.*

So there it is, some of what it means to be good, responsible parents regardless of how things turn out. But what *about* how things turn out? How much of what we do really influences how each of our children turns out in terms of personality, intelligence, interests, commitments, and character?

A great deal, say some parents who embrace conventional wisdom and expert advice. Not much say other parents who have raised at least two children. Consider the opinion of one such parent.

I am a single father who began raising two babies at the age of 42. I read all the "how to raise kids" books that I could find. Took parenting classes, etc. I was amazed, dismayed, and eventually heartbroken to see how my two kids chose their own destructive destiny despite my nurturing efforts. They continually made poor choices in all areas of their lives. The result was that both of my children are in the juvenile justice system. I have the advantage of being older and have made numerous observations of family and friends. Parenting techniques seem to have absolutely nothing to do with a child's behavior. If anything, children actually influence the parents. I noticed this phenomena when I was a teenager, myself. You almost have to experience it to understand it.

Does this challenging comment apply to the average child or better yet, to our child? Between the push of heredity and the pull of peers, do we parents really have so little control over how our children turn out in so many ways? Yes, says the most famous psychologist of all time.

The [biological] foundation has so much the upper hand over personal accidental experience that it makes no difference whether a child has sucked at the breast, or has been brought up on the bottle and never enjoyed the tenderness of a mother's care. In both cases, the child's development takes the same path.

That Sigmund Freud would wind up saying such a thing is truly amazing. After all, more than any other psychologist he and his followers successfully promoted the idea that parenting during the early childhood makes a profound difference to how a child's personality develops.

Increasingly, modern psychologists familiar with the best science are saying the same thing that Freud said about the power of a child's biology:

Nowadays parents are told that spankings will make their children more aggressive, that criticism will destroy their self-esteem, and that children who feel loved will be kinder and more loving to others. As a result of this advice, most parents today are administering far fewer spankings and reprimands, and far more physical affection and praise, than their grandparents did.

Perhaps the "experts" don't know what they're talking about. Perhaps parenting styles are less important than people have been led to believe. Perhaps human nature is more robust than most people give it credit for—perhaps children are designed to resist whatever their parents do to them. It's possible that being hit by a parent doesn't make children want to go right out and hit their playmates, any more than being kissed by a parent makes them want to go right out and kiss their playmates. It's even possible (dare I suggest it?) that those parents who are still doling out a lot of punishment have aggressive kids because aggressiveness is, in part, passed on genetically.

Strong words, indeed, that make us wonder: Can this biological view be mostly true? My wife Leslie and I believed the likely answer was yes, given all the compelling evidence. Nevertheless, we often ignored what we knew while going for broke with affection, enrichment, and demands for good conduct that good parents do for their kids. Well, of course, it was only natural for us to do so.

But let's face it: there are feelings and there is reality. Let's say we parents can never really know just how much of our children's development reflects their interactions with us and how much reflects their own biology. I say fine, as long as we are clear about two things.

First, *no credible biological view can deny the importance of quality parenting and family values.* But secondly, *no credible social view can deny the power of biology to limit what parents and family life can accomplish.* It's high time we confronted head-on and with an open mind what our best science has revealed about that power of biology to limit a parent's influence.

Chapter 6
Parenting Straight Up

Actress Lauren Bacall once explained how her relationships with men were shaped by personal loss. Her father disappeared two years after her parents divorced, when she was eight.

"My mother put out everything for me, and he gave nothing. Somewhere, unconsciously that must have affected my feelings about men, my basic distrust of a relationship with a man being able to last any length of time . . . . I felt deserted by my father, certainly, which was an actual fact. We all grow up with scars, and that scared me when I was young, and from that time on I always dreamed of all these wonderful fairy tales, those wonderful stories of when the prince comes along, and saves you, and I was very, very insecure . . . . Maybe that has to do with having an incomplete family, being an only child."

Perhaps so. Divorce or desertion can be traumatic. For a while, anxiety and anger take over, with feelings of insecurity and a sense of betrayal. All this can drive some children into self-destructive relationships with equally troubled peers. The more rebellious they become, the more their school performance suffers.

Yet what about over a lifetime? I mean, does the break-up of a little girl's family explain why, once grown to womanhood, she tends to have emotional difficulties with men? If so for some women, then how do we explain such difficulties in women who never experienced such a break-up? Should we blame their healthy family life and loving parents? I dare say, we wouldn't.

So how can we know if either woman's emotional troubles really came from what her parents did or failed to do when she was growing up? We can speculate till the cows come home, yet to what end when, for any person, we can never really know?

Still we readily embrace explanations that make the most sense to us, giving no thought to other possibilities. But what if another possibility is the better explanation?

So consider two identical twins separated during infancy and reared in different adoptive homes. Amy was reared by lower-middle class parents with traditional beliefs in the value of self-restraint and education. The mother was socially awkward, over-weight, and insecure. She felt alienated by her pretty daughter's blond, blue-eyed features. She and her husband considered Amy a problem child, and so she was.

Right from the beginning Amy was anxious and demanding. Her insecurity showed up, for instance, in bed wetting, fear of the dark and of being alone, and frequent nightmares. By late child-hood she was shy, abnormally immature, and socially indifferent. She also suffered from a serious learning disorder. Dr. Peter Neubauer described Amy as a classic example of the rejected child. Her story fits the traditional idea that the quality of a child's upbringing makes a big difference to how that child turns out.

If that sounds perfectly reasonable, consider Amy's sister. Beth was raised by loving, cheerful, self-confident parents who delighted in their adoptive daughter. She had all the advantages of love, support, material possessions, and encouragement that Amy never had. Yet in many ways Beth's development mirrored Amy's almost exactly.

Right from the beginning, she too showed the same insecurity as Amy. Beth was a thumb sucker, a nail biter, a bed wetter, and a blanket clencher. Like Amy, she was afraid of the dark and of being left alone. According to Dr. Neubauer, "She too became lost in role-playing, and the artificial nature of her personality was even more pronounced than Amy's."

If twins are mostly like all children, then such anecdotes sug-gest a basic truth about our children's development. *Every child's inborn potential, normal or abnormal, tends to unfold in its own way.* Social pressure from parents and peers will influence such unfolding, no doubt.

Identical twins reared apart learn and do different things. They may even speak different languages and believe in different gods. Yet they do so with similar energy, intelligence, and mood. One twin might be a liberal, the other a conservative. One might be a Christian, the other a Jew. Yet both will show similar commitment to their politics or religion, however passionate or casual it may be.

Amy and Beth grew up in different families. Since their genes are identical, only their different social environments—different parents, siblings, friends, peers—could easily explain any psychological differences they might display. So it stands to reason that large psychological differences between any identical twins reared apart must reflect strong social influence while small psychological differences between them must reflect weak social influence.

Well, what do we find with such twins? We find mostly *small psychological differences suggesting weak social influence.* For some traits, for example, agreeableness, conscientiousness, extroversion, we find hardly any difference at all! So much psychological similarity for genetic identicals raised in different homes with different friends and school environments: how remarkable!

For illustration, consider intelligence as measured by the usual IQ tests. From IQ studies we learn two interesting things. First, identicals brought up by different parents are almost as alike in IQ as identicals brought up by the same parents; *this reveals the power of genetic influence.* But second, neither group is perfectly alike. Rather, they are merely similar. This reveals the limits of genetic influence. Together, these two facts about identical-twin IQ make clear that *genes aren't everything.* They *are* something, indeed, but not everything!

That identical twins reared apart are as similar on IQ tests as identicals reared together is as stunning a finding as any in all of psychology. Yet there is more. A similar rule applies to many personality traits, for instance, how sociable, anxious, or aggressive the twins tend to be. Concerning such traits, identicals brought up by different parents are almost as alike as identicals brought up by the same parents.

Okay, we've considered *genetically identical* siblings (twins) who are brought up by different parents. But what about *genetically unrelated* siblings (adoptees) brought up by the same parents? Since they are genetically unrelated, any psychological similarities must reflect their shared social environment of parents, siblings, peers, and schooling. So again, it stands to reason that striking psychological similarities must mean strong social influence while weak psychological similarities must mean weak social influence.

Well, what do we find? We find either *small psychological similarities suggesting weak social influence, or modest psychological similarities that mostly disappear by adulthood, suggesting impermanent social influence.*

In short, adoptively related (genetically unrelated) siblings are in many ways remarkably different while identical twins reared apart are in many ways remarkably alike.

Both these observations carry the same message. Many qualities our children show for a lifetime come much more from the genes they possess than the parenting they experienced. It means our children's "family resemblance" for many traits reflects their shared heredity more than their shared parenting.

This stunning fact of family life challenges conventional wisdom about the great influence of parenting techniques during a child's "formative years." But if our way of parenting doesn't explain our children's similarities, how can we be sure it explains their differences? And if they don't really explain either, what then?

Can it really be that this or that way we go about parenting matters so little to many qualities that characterize our child's personality and prospects? If so, it may seem a bit unfair, considering all we do to engender the same good things in all our children.

With all of them, we encourage the same values and virtues, the same standards for personal conduct and achievement.

So yes, we naturally wonder can it truly be that all this has so little long-term impact? Apparently so, yet in other ways, maybe not. Consider the difference between what our children *are* and what they *do*. Our children's hearts and minds are one thing, their social behavior quite another. We may hardly influence certain personal traits, as we have just seen. But what about our children's social conduct?

To find out, we ask that familiar question about the family environment our children share. How much does it make them more similar to each other than to other children? Earlier, we asked about similarity in personality, intelligence, and mental health. Here, we ask about similarity in social conduct. So let's take a look, for example, at "religious orthodoxy," which involves two traits. One is *religiosity*, or depth of religious conviction. The other is *religious practice*, including choice of church and attendance at religious services. What do twin studies suggest?

Just this. A shared environment does help make siblings even more similar than their genes already make them. However, this is true for their religious practice more than their religiosity, that is for their conduct more than their conviction. Likewise for other kinds of social conduct. For instance, when it comes to delinquent behavior during adolescence, the environments siblings share can have as much influence as the genes they share, maybe even more.

So there it is: common sense confirmed, at least regarding social conduct. Sharing an environment does make our children similar to each other and therefore different from other children. But wait a minute. Exactly what kind of shared environment are the twin studies telling us about?

We naturally assume it's the shared *family* environment that molds our children's social habits during their "formative years."

77

Yet what if it's the shared *peer* environment that matters more? What if much of the influence we once had mostly fades as peer influence comes into play? So which is it, parents or peers? Which has the greater influence not just on how our children behave in different settings, but how they turn out regardless of settings?

I'm afraid we really can't be certain because twin studies typically don't separate family and peer influences. Rather, they just lump them together as social influence. With such lumping, it seems to me, we wind up with two rather unsatisfying messages about the "shared environment."

Message 1
Where the long-term influence of a shared environment proves weak—as with traits of personality, intelligence, and mental health—we can be reasonably certain that both our influence and peer influences are weak.

Message 2
Where the long-term influence of a shared environment is substantial—as with habits of conduct—we cannot be reasonably certain whether it is our influence or peer influence that matters more.

What a strange fact of family life all this suggests. *It seems we can be most certain where our influence is weakest, while least certain where our influence might be strongest!*

Not great news if we must accept both these messages. But must we? Perhaps we have overlooked something. In the next chapter, let's consider what that something might be.

Chapter 7
Parenting with a Twist

Family life involves conflict and negotiation. We parents bring to the table our unique personalities, parenting techniques, and rules for behavior. Our children bring their unique temperaments, talents, and needs. Each reacts differently to the other. Bargaining occurs and compromises are made.

Try as we may to be "fair and equal," we still respond differently to each child, as we should. Even if we could be truly even-handed, each child would still experience us differently. As one woman said, "My older brother and I frequently talk about my father, who died in 1968. You'd think we were talking about two totally different men!"

The comment is important for what it suggests about our influence. Much of it doesn't act similarly on all our children to make them similar. Rather, it interacts differently with each to make them different. Any influence we do have must therefore greatly depend on their personalities as well as ours. A little "monkey business" can help illustrate the point.

About 15 percent of rhesus monkeys are timid, right from infancy. During brief separations from their mother, for example, they have trouble eating and sleeping. They stay put rather than try to look for their mother. Even after she returns, they remain anxious.

Timid monkeys reared by strict foster mothers grow up to be emotionally skittish and socially inhibited. Often they wind up being victimized by everyone. Timid monkeys reared by nurturing foster mothers also grow up to be timid. Yet they act much more confidently where protective adults keep watch. In these safe situations, some even wind up dominating their peers! Thus can the same personality trait show up in strikingly different ways. Apparently, it's the same for children.

Like monkeys, 15 percent of children are shy and inhibited, right from infancy. Their timid nature shows up in anxiety about being alone or with unfamiliar people. It shows up in their higher heart rate, blood pressure, muscle tension, and stress hormone levels. It even shows up in the larger diameters of their pupils. Yet also like monkeys, timid children can be surprisingly confident in reasonably secure circumstances. Moreover, the older they get, the more confident and sociable most of them become.

Like some monkeys, some children are fearless, right from infancy. They either seem insensitive or don't react well to punishment. According to psychologist David Lykken, punishment works by fear of future punishment, and these children are too fearless to care. Frustrated parents naturally intensify their demands and reprimands. That's their job, and it works reasonably well with most children most of the time.

Not so with others whose willfulness defies the best efforts of parents. With them, the unintended effect of such vigorous parenting can be a rebellious child preferring the environment of peers, popular culture, and delinquent life style. Yet, says Lykken, that same child might have a different destiny had his parents relied "less on punishment and more on cultivating in the child a sense of pride. That kid may turn out to be a hero."

To me all this sounds easier said than done. Still, Lykken's message about antisocials is interesting for what it suggests for most children. It's not just that children with different antisocial potentials will behave differently, depending on how their parents treat them in this or that situation. Rather, it's that even children with the *same* antisocial potential can turn out different, *at least in the way they behave,* depending on how their parents bring them up.

All this makes good sense. After all, we've seen that genes aren't everything and that, beyond any inborn differences, social conditions, including parenting, do affect conduct. So again, let's distinguish where we can make the most difference, as with social conduct, and where we seem to make the least difference, as with personality and intelligence. It's the latter traits that have mainly concerned us. It is with these that we have repeatedly discovered the surprising limits of what we parents can make happen. It's with them that we face yet another mind-boggling idea about our lifetime influence.

The first one we considered in the last chapter:

• *Treating our children alike doesn't make them much more alike in many ways than they would otherwise have been.*

The second one we've been tackling in this chapter:

• *Treating each of our children differently doesn't make them much less alike in many ways than they would have been otherwise.*

Well then, what if both "mind-boggling ideas" proved mostly true? What if the similarities and differences in personality and other traits that our children carry with them into adulthood are mostly outside our control? Even so, it would not mean that we parents "count zilch," as some have claimed.

Yet again, it seems well to re-emphasize what should by now be clear: that we have all kinds of influence on our children, and not just on how they behave while they are in our care. For one thing, we can help shape the direction of their social conduct. For another, we leave them with a residue of memories, knowledge, and useful skills, and with lasting feelings ranging from love, respect, and gratitude to anger, resentment, and dread. Any or all of such feelings can be strong and can complicate family relationships for a lifetime.

Isaac Asimov, author of 500 books on everything from science fiction to guides to Shakespeare and the Bible, describes how he became a compulsive writer. His Russian-born father owned a succession of candy stores in Brooklyn that were open from 6 A.M. to 1 A.M. seven days a week. Young Isaac got up at 6 o'clock every morning to deliver papers and rushed home from school to help out in the store every afternoon. If he was even a few minutes late, his father yelled at him for being a *folyack*, Yiddish for sluggard. More than 50 years later, he wrote in his autobiography: "It is a point of pride with me that though I have an alarm clock, I never set it, but get up at 6 A.M. anyway. I am still showing my father I'm not a folyack."

As I suggested earlier, such memories and feelings will depend on how we handle major concerns that every child has about (a) challenging situations involving, for instance, sibling rivalry, parental conflict, parental drug use, or peer pressure; (b) emotional stress involving anxiety, envy, anger, despair; (c) self-confidence, especially doubts about fitting in socially and performing academically; (d) personality traits and personality changes involving secretiveness, emotional withdrawal, hostility; (e) moral questions involving honesty, loyalty, obligation, entitlement, justice, honor; and finally (f) ultimate questions about life, death, and God.

Yes, parenting has its lifelong effects on memories and feelings, as well as many other things. Yet we have seen that parenting, however good it is, has surprisingly limited influence on many lifetime traits. Resistance to change in these traits means that, in a way, our influence on our children is a lot like our influence on each other.

We know, for example, that spouses try to get each other to change in one way or another: "Quit acting like such a . . . ." "Can't you be more . . . .?" Yet despite all such efforts, spouses wind up resembling each other in personality no more after 30 or 40 years of marriage than at the beginning! Of course, their emotional reactions to each other and, consequently, their relationship do change over the years, in some cases quite dramatically.

As it is with our spouses, so it is with each of us and each of our children. And what do these differences say about our powers to influence the kind of person our child turns out to be? A father of two boys writes:

> Ryan and Jeff are so different I think it must be genetic because they were raised in the same environment and in the same way. Jeff's room—well, you need to be agile to walk through it without breaking something. It's controlled chaos with garbage, money, books, magazines everywhere. Ryan's room must always be in order. He vacuums his room every week. Jeff is not interested in working to make money, and he didn't save a dollar when he did work. Ryan is materialistic. He has the first nickel he made. He has saved money, and his checking account grew even when he didn't work.
>
> Jeff wants to be a screenwriter. Ryan wants to be an electrical engineer. Jeff is real laid back. Ryan is impatient and sometimes aggressive. Jeff's idea of a good time is to go to the coffee shop. Ryan's idea of a good time is going to the gym. Looking back, I don't really think you can change . . . a person's predisposition—same with patience, you just can't teach it.

Moral of the story? Those two "mind-boggling ideas" don't deny our influence on our children's social conduct. Neither do they deny the legacy of teachings, memories, and feelings we leave our children. Rather they deny only that this legacy greatly determines the kind of person they are and the kind of person they will become.

This in turn suggests something that may be hard to accept, even if we suspect it is true. Despite all the obvious influences we do have, *our children would likely turn out more or less the same in many of their personal qualities even if raised by other parents.*

If this seems like an unhappy thought, consider another, more hopeful thought. Despite all, they remain *our* children. Their lives are entwined with our lives, not with other parents' lives. Their memories, their interests, their loves and hates, are about us and the world we help make for them, not about others and other worlds. In this sense, they are truly ours, part of us, for now and always. And that makes all the difference.

* * *

No doubt then, our children's development depends on many influences beyond our control. The genetic kind we'll consider shortly. The environmental kind, including some we hardly ever think about, we'll look at now. Indeed, when it comes to our children's development, genes are most definitely *not* everything!

When we hear "environment," we naturally think of parents, family life, peers, schooling, and culture. We hardly ever think of wombs. *Yet the prenatal world of the womb is just as "environmental" as the social world.* Moreover, any influence it does have will be different for each child. Therefore, different *prenatal* experiences could help make our children even less alike than their different genes and social experiences already make them, though by how much is anyone's guess.

Obviously, parents influence their children's social environment. But what about a parent influencing a child's prenatal experience? That is, could some of a parent's behavior influence a child's psychological development by affecting that child's prenatal experience? A confident answer is hard to come by. So again let's look for clues in some unusual cases.

In the 1950s, some pregnant women took a synthetic hormone called DES (diethylstilbestrol) to prevent miscarriage. The treatment worked but there was an unforeseen side effect. Many female offspring of these pregnancies became tomboys. They preferred cars and trucks over dolls, competition over cooperation, competitive rough-and-tumble play over quiet talk, and blue jeans over frilly dresses. As one observer put it, "Their dolls may stay on the shelf from Christmas to Christmas, but not their cowboy gear, toy cars, and guns." Whatever the social influence, prenatal hormones had clearly made a big difference.

Normally, the prenatal world is mostly out of a parent's control, yet not entirely. A mother's diet, the drugs she takes, her emotional state affected by family life: any of these can affect prenatal conditions, for better or worse. Here's an example of a "worse" case.

Throughout her pregnancy, my wife drank, sometimes enough to induce an altered state of being. We later found out she has genetic alcoholic tendencies, and subsequently six years later, needed to be placed in an alcoholic recovery program.

Jack began having seizures with moderate fevers as early as age two. So he was placed on low dosages of dilantin for about three years. I was convinced that his seizures were caused by all that drinking and smoking my wife did while she was pregnant with him.

When he entered kindergarten and first grade, Jack exhibited aggressive behaviors toward other children in his class. Often he hit them or threw rocks at their heads. I remember in second grade receiving a call from the principal informing me of child being injured by Jack's rock throwing. Most of the children made fun of him, and of course he had few friends.

We tried to get him interested in sports, but his attention span was never focused enough. In soccer, he would just sit in the middle of the field while the other children would be involved in the game around him. The coach would talk to him, but he wouldn't move. Eventually, he was physically removed from the game, which I feel is what he wanted.

Although he was quite intelligent, his grades in school were poor. He never took the time to study. He would quickly lose focus in any project. When he was six, his mother and I divorced and she moved with Jack to Florida. His behavior with her only got worse. At age 12, he stole her car and wound up wrecking it. After a psychological evaluation, he was sent to a special school for problem children. After four months, he complained so much he was asked to leave.

While extreme, such stories accurately illustrate how prenatal factors might limit or magnify normal parenting influences. We know, for example, that smoking and drinking during a pregnancy can stress a fetal brain. Pregnant women who smoke at least 10 cigarettes a day put their offspring at special risk. When toddlers, more of them are extremely impulsive and rebellious. When older, more of them have conduct problems, the sons with delinquent and violent behavior, the daughters with drug abuse. Any kind of child abuse, neglect, or other destructive conditions at home can make such outcomes more likely and more devastating.

Yet fetal stress can occur for reasons other than a mother's behavior or the quality of home life. It might be a seemingly random viral infection, a defect in the umbilical cord or some other fluke of nature. Whatever the source, how can we know if prenatal stress has even occurred? We typically can't be sure. Yet we can look to certain tell-tale signs displayed by the newborn that might give us a hint.

One is a defect in the umbilical cord. Other tell-tale signs are slightly odd physical traits such as low set ears, fly-away hair, a curved pinkie finger, or unusual spaces between the toes. Still others involve a difference between the left and right side of the body, for example, in the size or location of ears or in the number of fingerprint ridges.

Such signs can be found in many of us. It's just that they are more striking and numerous in people with medical or psychiatric disorders, and in children at high risk of becoming violent adults. All this suggests that prenatal stress can make a child, especially a genetically vulnerable child, even more vulnerable to the influence of poor parenting.

That's the bad news but there is some good news too. For such vulnerable children, the quality of the parenting they get may make some difference. Apparently, their chance of getting into trouble is less likely if their parents are reasonably well adjusted and the home life is relatively normal.

All these examples along with new scientific findings suggest how our children's unique biology might exaggerate or limit our influence. In this chapter we considered some social and prenatal aspects of that biology. In the next we'll consider some of its genetic aspects.

Chapter 8
Beyond Parenting

"Where did we go wrong?" This plaintive question comes from Mrs. Meant-Well, a discouraged mother of an emotionally disturbed daughter. It's a question asked by many a long-suffering parent. A forceful answer comes from the late columnist Ann Landers. "Stop berating yourselves. You did your best, now let it rest. I've seen parents who were alcoholic, neglectful and irresponsible, but their children turned out extremely well. There's no perfect formula for successful parenthood—at least I don't know of it."

The idea that genes have a significant effect troubles some people, yet comforts others. I suspect that Mrs. Meant-Well was comforted by Mrs. Lander's ringing defense of all "meant-well" parents. She writes:

Some children turn out to be champions in spite of parents who provided precious little emotional nourishment, while other kids—loved, wanted, tenderly nurtured, with all the supposed advantages—turn out perverse, estranged, and unable to cope. I have come to believe in the genetic factor, which has been ignored by many behavioral "experts." We all inherit our nervous system and if our nervous system is fragile, it places severe limitations on what a person can tolerate. Certain people are born survivors. They can withstand life's harshest blows and emerge the stronger for it. Others crumble in the face of minor adversity. The same fire that melts butter can make steel stronger.

This message rests on scientific findings as well as amazing stories about identical twins brought up by different parents. In all of the evidence, we recognize the power of genetic influence. Indeed, but what kind of influence are we talking about? To keep things simple, let's consider just one, the kind that's like the sound of an orchestra. With an orchestra, the more musicians, the more imposing the sound. Likewise, the more genes for a trait, the more imposing that trait will be. In other words, each gene's little influence adds up, and in identical twins, it adds up in the same way.

All this partly explains why some people whose genes for this or that trait add up to a lot more than normal are therefore more sociable, adventurous, and energetic than others. It partly explains why some people are kinder, more affectionate, or calmer and more stable than others. It also partly explains why still others are more callous or compulsive, suspicious or socially withdrawn, or more angry or anxious than others.

Genes can affect our sense of well-being. They can affect our risk for alcoholism and heavy smoking, eating disorders, and obesity. They can even affect the strength of our attitudes, values, and religious interests. Look at it this way: Our behavior reveals who has more and who has less than our "fair share" of certain genes.

The adding up of genes could even explain something else about us and our children. We all contain within our personalities inconsistent, sometimes clashing qualities that can make us so interesting to others, even mysterious, and sometimes hard to predict. We seem to be a "haphazard bundle of inconsistent qualities," says writer Somerset Maugham:

> I have known crooks who were capable of self-sacrifice, sneak-thieves who were sweet-natured and harlots for whom it was a point of honour to give good value for money . . . Selfishness and kindliness, idealism and sensuality, vanity, shyness, disinterestedness, courage, laziness, nervousness, obstinacy, and diffidence, they can all exist in a single person and form a plausible harmony . . . . I find that the longer I know people the more they puzzle me.

In short, the adding up of genes could explain not just differences between us and our children but different tendencies within our own personality. It could explain why some of our deepest conflicts are as much with ourself—should I say our *selves*?—as they are with others.

Remember that half of a child's genes are the same, on average, as those of a parent or sibling. It's this gene sharing that promotes family resemblance. It's the main reason that many traits run in families. Tall parents tend to have tall children and overweight parents tend to have overweight children. Bright parents tend to have bright children and musically talented parents tend to have musically inclined children. It's the same with emotionally troubled parents and their children, and with antisocial parents and their children. Yet here's something more interesting.

Gene sharing can make us and any of our children show unusually strong resemblance. Remember, we share half of their genes, *on average*. This means that, strictly by chance, we and any of our children might share more genes than average for a particular trait, skill, or interest.

Such sharing could explain why a mother's involvement in art or music occurs in one of her daughters, but not in the others. Could it explain even a striking resemblance like those shown by identical twins? My next-door neighbor's story illustrates the point:

Jim and Kim married in 1972 and moved next door. Jim was an advertising account executive and Kim was on the faculty of the medical school. In February 1976, Kim gave birth to a boy whom they named Jim Jr.

A year and a half later, in July of 1977, Kim came over and asked if we knew where Jim was. We didn't. Kim said that she had come home from work the day before only to find all of Jim's personal belongings gone. Kim next heard from Jim in August when he filed for divorce. Neither Kim nor Jim Jr. ever saw or spoke to Jim since that day in July. Kim never discussed Jim or his personal habits with Jr. She never told Jr. that Jim was in advertising.

Jr. is now 24 and the spitting image of Jim. He smokes Salem cigarettes, just as Jim did, despite Kim being a zealous anti-smoking crusader. Jr. works for an advertising agency, as did Jim. Perhaps strangest of all is that Jr., just as Jim did, keeps his change in his left pocket and when he gets nervous, he jingles the change in a somewhat annoying manner!

Jr. was living with his high school sweetheart for the past 3 years. Just last week, the girl came home to find that Jr. had taken all of his personal belongings and moved to an undisclosed location. He hasn't even told his mother where he is currently living.

Like so many others, this little story reminds us that gene sharing can explain why children seem to rediscover for themselves some of what their parents discovered in themselves years earlier.

One day when he was 23, my son showed me a large maze he had drawn at about age 12. You can see in miniature one quarter

of it, on the left. It's rather complex, for instance, with "road guides" that either allow or frustrate a player's effort to locate keys that open locks. (You may need a magnifying glass to see the tiny arrow in the lower left corner that points to one such key.)

Suddenly inspired, I rummaged through my old stuff and bingo! There it was, a maze I had drawn when I too was about 12. You can see a quarter of it, also in miniature, on the right.

What really bowled me over was not the obvious differences—you can tell which one of us is the computer genius! No, what really bowled me over was the similar complexity of these mazes, including the same rule that a player must locate a key along a path to the goal!

Who could have predicted that the little two-year-old boy who drew that big-head person (Chapter 1) and a little later the following "family portrait," would turn into a math maven and gift-

ed computer programmer? How unpredictable our children's development may prove to be! Incidentally, I challenge you to figure out why the "Daddy" figure is so small. (Hint: there are at least two possibilities.)

My little anecdote about father and son mazes suggests that our child's resemblance to us may sometimes have less to do with how we are now than how we were years ago. It's why, for example, an adolescent girl's delinquent behavior may have much more in common with her mother's adolescent behavior than with her mother's current behavior. A therapist offers this example.

A teenager in my practice was an honor student, a compliant girl, popular, and busy with many extracurricular activities. Yet, she was always somewhat emotional and impulsive. She tended to be argumentative, bossy with peers, mildly disorganized in her problem solving. But she was smart, pretty, and friendly.

Puberty hits, and she became chronically irritable, angry, emotionally unstable. She no longer fit into her "good/preppy" crowd. Gradually she fell into the more troubled "gangster/druggy" group. She couldn't concentrate and got frustrated in school, so she no longer went. She acted out sexually with older men, got pregnant, had an abortion, felt guilty, and become deeply depressed.

Her parents are stunned. They never imagined such problems with her. Yet, on close inspection with the family, we discover something interesting. The mother reports similar events in her own adolescence, including an abortion.

Like wine, our genes take time to mature. Before they do, though, we may have no clue to what's in store. We recognize the mysterious unfolding of genetic influence in changes that come with puberty. We can appreciate how it explains why a mother and daughter might go through a similar phase at about the same age. "She's doing just what I did when I was her age!"

The influence of genes in typical family life seems convincing enough. It seems even more convincing for adoptive family life. *Adopted children resemble the biological parents they've never known more than the adoptive parents they've known all their lives.*

Biologist Jonathan Weiner tells of a friend reared by adoptive parents. The friend had finally tracked down her biological mother and invited her for a visit.

On the day [the mother] arrived they stayed up talking late into the night. Finally everyone went to bed. But at around three in the morning my friend woke up. She often got hungry in the middle of the night, and was in the habit of making plain spaghetti at two or three in the morning. She decided to go down to the kitchen . . . . To her astonishment, she found her mother standing by the stove, boiling a pot of spaghetti. "That's how I knew she was my mother," my friend said. "She ate spaghetti in the middle of the night, just like me."

Genetic influence can explain family resemblance, but also family differences. Recall that a child and a parent share half of their genes, on average. Yet again, strictly by chance, they might share fewer genes than average for any one trait, skill, or interest. This could explain why in many specific ways we can have surprisingly little in common with our children.

We might have many of the genes for some trait and therefore show it while any one of our children has few of them and therefore doesn't show it. On the other hand, we might have few of the genes for some trait and therefore don't show it while any one of our children has many of them and therefore does show it. Here's why this might be important for some parents.

Consider two loving, law-abiding parents with a daughter who is persistently anxious and depressed or a son who is incorrigibly rebellious and antisocial. The mother and father each could have some "neurotic" genes or "antisocial" genes, yet not enough to cause either one any problems. In other words, each parent is a "silent carrier" of a weak genetic potential.

Now imagine that, completely by chance, one of their children inherits a "double dose" of that hidden potential—one from the father and one from the mother. The two small doses add up to a big dose and therefore a strong disposition. In this way, two normal parents can have a troubled child despite their best efforts.

With little appreciation of such genetic influence, the parents might easily blame themselves. "What did we do wrong? Where did we fail?" They might easily blame the environment. "He got in with the wrong crowd!" Yet we have seen just how far from the mark each of these explanations might be.

With adoptive parents and their adoptive children, genetic sharing isn't just modest for some traits. Generally, it's just about zero for all traits. Such non-sharing can make them as different as strangers. The point is nicely illustrated by the following rather extreme anecdote.

A professional couple with three bright boys decides to adopt an infant girl. As it often happens, they do so without information on the biological parents. Still, they naturally expect that the highly stimulating environment of their family will encourage the same high intelligence in their adopted child as shown by their biological children. Yet the child's intelligence proves to be below normal.

How do highly cultured, IQ-140 parents interested in science, politics, and the arts relate to an IQ-90 child with no such intellectual capability or motivation? How, indeed, when a 50-point mental gulf is all but impossible to bridge. How sad the child's sense of being a stranger in the family . . . .

A big difference like this could just as well involve the reverse, as the following equally extreme anecdote illustrates.

An infant boy is adopted by simple country, backwoods folk. Their book shelf held only a bible, a tractor's manual, and phone directory. Gradually, the boy shows an increasing desire to read lots of books. Later, he gets a library card and starts reading. Eventually, he goes to college, which no one from his village had ever done. Conscious of his difference from his parents and every one else in the village, he becomes curious to know of his biological relatives. After much digging, he discovers that many of them were intellectuals with university degrees. His biological parents had been students. When his mother became pregnant, she and the father gave him up for adoption.

These rather extreme anecdotes illuminate what is generally true but easily missed, that "family resemblance" for many life-long traits depend a lot on shared genes, while differences in family members depend a lot on differences in their genes. It could even involve a difference in where genes come from. Now there's a strange statement I'd better explain.

Boys normally have one "X" and one "Y," or "male," chromosome in each of their cells. Genetically, boys are "XY." Girls normally have two "X," or "female," chromosomes in every cell in their body. Genetically, girls are "XX." Well, not always.

Occasionally, a girl is born with only one X in each of her cells. Such "single-X girls" are "XO." Now you might wonder why such a fluke of nature might be relevant. Yet twinning too is a fluke of nature, and it has revealed a lot about us and our children. So then, does the XO condition likewise reveal something interesting? Apparently yes, and not just something interesting but something really spectacular, if we can believe it.

Because "single-X girls" have only one X chromosome, they tend to have short stature, an immature little-girl appearance, and an inability to bear children. Yet because they have no Y chromosome, they are usually feminine in their behavior and in the way they think about themselves. For instance, they enjoy playing with dolls or caring for babies, and look forward to romance, marriage, pregnancy, and motherhood.

Now here's what's most fascinating about these girls. Compared to those who inherit their single X from their father, those who inherit their single X from their mother are more troubled and difficult for their parents and teachers to manage. For one thing, they are less skillful at reading other people's feelings. For another, they tend to be more demanding, more irrational when upset, and generally more likely to act in socially inappropriate ways.

Apparently, such differences are so evident that one investigator could make this extraordinary observation. "We've gotten to the point where we can make a pretty good guess of where a girl's chromosome came from just by knowing about her social behavior." How strange. Why should it matter whether an X chromosome is inherited from a mother or a father? Finally, what does any of this tell us about why our children are the way they are?

Here's one possible answer to both questions. Certain genes on the X chromosome promote proper social behavior, *but only if those genes are active*. Trouble is, they aren't active. Rather, they are switched off if they are riding on the X chromosome that comes from a mother. This is "bad news" for those single-X girls who get their single X from their mother.

Likewise it's "bad news" for boys since they too get a single X from their mother along with a Y from their father. Normal girls, on the other hand, get an X from their mother but also an X from their father. So girls get plenty of those "good" active genes from their father, while boys do not.

Do the "switched off" genes on the X chromosome that boys get from their mother help explain why they are socially less mature than girls? Does it explain why boys seem like "frogs and snails and puppy dogs' tails"? And what about girls? Do active genes on the X chromosome girls get from their father help explain why they seem like "sugar and spice and everything nice"? At this point, no one can say for certain, though I like to think there's something to it.

Can it be true that moms have a hidden power to prenatally switch off certain "good" genes on their X chromosome? No one knows how or why, but then again many things in nature remain mysterious. So yes, in this case you might say that moms are in some sense "responsible" but not consciously and therefore not to blame for being such a "turn off."

The important message here is the familiar one. *Some things just happen for "no good reason." They aren't anyone's personal doing and they aren't anyone's fault.* Much about our children, including their social maturity, must reflect more than simply the parenting we give them. It must also reflect the genes we give them, not just the usual kind we've come across so often but maybe a mysterious "switchable" kind as well.

* * *

All right, now we come to it: that most controversial of questions. *Of all influences making us and our children similar in some ways and different in other ways, how much is the genetic kind?* To say that genetic differences make a difference isn't saying a lot. To say *how much* they make a difference, well, that *is* saying a lot.

The relevant science is solid on this question and the findings are compelling. So then, how much of a difference do genetic differences really make, say between us and our children or among our children? Our best answer: quite a lot, though just how much will depend on the trait.

When it comes to differences in measured intelligence (IQ), genetic influence is surprisingly strong. During childhood, it's about 50 percent of all influences, rising thereafter to 75 percent by adulthood. (Yes, the genetic reason we differ in IQ does apparently increase as we get older.)

Yet IQ is merely part of an incredible story that says so much about why our children turn out they way they do. The story also includes a host of traits, normal and abnormal. Differences, for instance, in how susceptible we are to major mental disorders reflect strong genetic influence.

Of all influences that make some people more likely than others to succumb to schizophrenia and bipolar disorder, over 70 percent are genetic. For other kinds of depression, it's about 30 percent and for some eating disorders related to depression, it's about 50 percent. For alcoholism, it's about 55 percent and for drug abuse it's over 60 percent.

Why children differ in their disposition to abuse drugs and to behave antisocially may involve genetic influence as high as 40 to 75 percent. It may be an even bigger reason—about 80 percent—why some children are severely hyperactive.

Finally, the reason for childhood autism may be as much as 90 percent genetic. This fact is particularly interesting, given that parents have often been blamed for causing this illness by their cold personalities and rejection of the child. What a cruel joke, accusing hapless parents of perpetrating a terrible mental illness that is actually rooted in their child's biology.

There's a lot more to the remarkable story of genetic influence. Genetic differences between people help explain our children's diverse *abilities*, for instance, for athletics or with mechanical devices. And it's the same with various *interests*, such as:

* woodworking or stamp collecting
* doing crossword puzzles
* religious activities
* scientific study
* reading and writing
* working outdoors
* riding roller coasters

* gambling and seeking adventure
* engaging in artistic and creative activity.

Likewise, we find genetic influence in *preferences*, say for the hand we favor when writing or brushing. We find it for the time of day we prefer to eat, for how much and what to eat, and for the number of eating companions we prefer.

Isn't that interesting? We hardly give such things a thought, never mind a second thought. Yet even these things are influenced by our genes. It may even be true for why some children often hold their breath until they get so pale or blue in the face that they may even lose consciousness! For such behavior, who ever thinks about genetic influence? Yet it seems that genes may have more than a little to do with it.

We find genetic influence in values regarding hard work and self-discipline, and in social *attitudes* toward censorship, divorce, abortion, and the death penalty. We find it even in such things as physical fitness and response to fitness training.

And, when it comes to why we differ in fatness or thinness, the story is similar. Between 40 and 80 percent of all influences are the genetic kind. Genetic influence is even a big reason why some of us become habitual cigarette smokers—about 40 percent—and even why we smokers differ in the number of cigarettes we smoke: perhaps 80 to 90 percent.

An especially interesting aspect of our story involves *personality* traits like extroversion, agreeableness, and emotional stability. Many studies have found genetic influence of roughly 50 percent, or even higher when ratings by peers are used as well as self-ratings. Incredibly, genetic influence is easily as high for a trait called "social responsibility." This one involves maturity, helping and sharing, living by moral principles, and a tendency to follow social norms.

If there's one trait that ought to reflect differences in rearing, this should be it, don't you think? Yet our best evidence suggests otherwise. For example, almost all differences among middle-class adolescents in "social responsibility" come from differences in their genes rather than from differences in how they were reared.

Given all this genetic influence on so many qualities, it's no wonder *we find genetic influence in parenting itself.* Still it's odd to think of parenting and other social influence as partly "nature," when we are so used to treating them as entirely "nurture." Yet what else can they be? After all, they do reflect personality, intelligence and many other genetically influenced qualities.

Only by thinking of parenting as "nature" as well as "nurture" can we understand two facts about how adult twins bring up their own children. First, the parenting styles used by identicals who grew up apart are as similar as the parenting styles used by identicals who grew up together. Second, this similarity in parenting, even for identicals who grew up apart, is greater than that for fraternals who grew up together.

These two facts suggest that the way our parents raised us doesn't much explain how we go about raising our own children. Apparently, we figure out how to do it, more from intuition inspired by our genes than from learning taught by our parents. We like to think of ourselves as our own person doing our own things with our own children, and rightly so! It's just that the best science we have says that "our own thing" is highly influenced by our own genes.

Now imagine we are doing our own thing and other parents are doing their own thing and, lo and behold, some of these "own things" turn out to be similar. For instance, most middle-class parents with middle-class values will try to encourage social responsibility in their children. Yet the children of such families still wind up quite different in how socially responsible they turn out. Similar rules yet different outcomes: Why? I'm guessing that by now you probably know.

Recall the most striking finding from that study of "social responsibility" in middle-class adolescents. Almost all the differences between them came from differences in their genes. None came from differences in how they were brought up by their parents. The inescapable conclusion? Genes strongly influence a child's *receptivity* to any parenting that encourages socially responsible attitudes and behavior. In that sense, our children really are running the show more than we think!

Clearly then, there is no guarantee that our best efforts to instill social responsibility will pan out. It's our job to try our best; of course we know that. Yet while we teach our children our own and society's rules, we cannot count on the proper learning taking place. For some children, it will happen; for others it won't. For still others, the learning will be a sometime thing: real but unreliable.

The bottom line: *There's a big difference between teaching and learning—what we try to instill and what sticks for the long haul.* We simply must recognize the difference if we are ever to understand the nature of the education that goes on in our homes.

There's just one last point about personality I would like to make here. It's about the power of personality to survive in spite of severe mental illness. Consider a study of identical twins reported by psychiatrist E. Fuller Torrey. "It didn't seem to matter that one twin had schizophrenia and the other didn't," he says. "If one twin was altruistic, so was the other. And if one was manipulative, the other was too." In many ways, he says, "they retained their underlying similarities."

Some of their similarities involved compelling coincidences that we sometimes discover in normal identical twins. A pair of twins, one normal, the other schizophrenic, bought a present in a gift shop. Neither twin knew that the other had done so. Only much later did they discover something as amusing as it was incredible. Each had purchased three boxes of note cards, two with the same designs! Apparently, not even disabling disease can wipe out what we truly are deep down.

I think the ravages of physical and mental disease are both superficial; that there is something unfathomably deep beyond their reach, that this is the best and strongest and realest thing we have; and that once upon a time this was called the Soul.

These inspiring words of psychiatrist Oliver Sacks capture beautifully what the scientific evidence is telling us about genetic influence on our lives and the lives of our children. When it comes to our personality, intelligence, interests, attitudes—even our quirks and goofy habits—we are mostly our own person, in large part because we are genetically unique.

"It's quite an astonishing possibility," said comedian Steve Allen, "that our genes may have a substantial influence on our behavior. Isn't it interesting to speculate that people behave as they do partly because of those little spheres of DNA that look like tapioca pudding in a glass dish. 'So, that explains why Uncle Louie is such a son of a bitch!' "

For some hard-nosed observers, all the findings we've explored support a radical view of child development, as expressed in this provocative comment by psychologist David Rowe:

Indeed, the best guess we could make about the psychological and physical traits of another person, without interviewing him or her directly, would be based upon the characteristics of the person's identical twin (if one could be found). Nothing we might discover about the conditions of rearing, schooling, neighborhood, religion, or school yard friends would come close to the usefulness of an identical twin in providing information about this person's height, weight, eye color, temperament, mental illness, habits, IQ, values or nearly any other trait.

Perhaps you are asking yourself, "Now what?" Do we just try to do what we think is best, hang on for the ride, and hope things will turn out for the best? What does all this evidence of genetic influence really mean?

I'll keep things as simple and conservative as possible. So let's first assume that of all influences that make each child's development unique, at least 50 percent are genetic. Fine, but what about the *other 50 percent?* How much of it involves our influence as parents? Truth be told, we can't be sure because our best science isn't clear. Still, we can make a few educated guesses.

First, some of that other 50 percent involves *physical events* that can alter brain activity and therefore personality and conduct. Such events can occur during prenatal life, as we have seen. It might occur later in life, for instance a head injury from a fight or accident—or even from a beating administered by an abusive parent or a nasty peer.

All right, let's allow that the combined influence of genes and physical conditions that affect the brain is 60 percent of all influences. That leaves 40 percent, but of what? Most of that 40 percent must involve social influence from parents and family life and from peers and popular culture. With our older children, the influence of peers and popular culture is mostly beyond our control. But what about *our* influence: how much of it, too, is mostly beyond our control?

If that sounds like an odd question, remember this. The give-and-take of normal family life is not simply a matter of a parent giving and a child taking, as we saw in Chapter 6 ("Parenting Straight Up"). Rather, a parent's give depends on a child's take, as we saw in Chapter 7 ("Parenting With A Twist"). And how strong is this *child-dependent* kind of parental influence? Again I have to say, we lack enough solid evidence to know for certain.

Yet one thing is certain: Our child is no empty vessel to be filled with our agenda. Rather, each comes into the world uniquely endowed in talents, temperament, and needs. Willful dispositions and social influences outside the family will inevitably clash with what parents try to make happen. Just how all this works out may involve developments we hardly imagined.

The handwriting is on the wall with a clear message about the limits of our influence. Why then is there still so much difficulty appreciating what the evidence says so convincingly? Indeed, why such difficulty even when our personal experience with our own children should underscore the truth? These questions are as important as any we've yet considered, mainly because of what the answers reveal about ourselves.

PART 3

FACTS AND FICTION
Beyond the Hokum and Hype

Chapter 9

Reflections of Nature

How do people normally explain why their children are the way they are? How do we explain why *we* are the way *we* are? Typically, we mostly go by our intuition, personal experience, and common sense. It's natural, we all do it all the time, confidently and with much satisfaction. Yet we've seen that with such explanations we risk deceiving ourselves about all sorts of things including ourselves and our children. A good example of such self-deception is this delightful anecdote told by Dr. Peter Neubauer:

> Two 30-year-old identical twins separated at birth and raised in different countries were asked about their personal habits. Interviewed separately, they both proved to be compulsively neat, precise, meticulous, punctual, and obsessed with cleanliness, all to pathological excess.
>
> Asked for an explanation, one twin answered, "My mother. When I was growing up, she kept the house perfectly ordered. She insisted on every little thing being returned to its proper place . . . . I learned from her. What else could I do?" Sounds convincing enough. Yet when asked the same question, the other twin answered, "The reason is quite simple. I'm reacting to my mother who is an absolute slob."

By itself, each twin's explanation makes perfect sense; each sounds like explanations we've all made at one time or another. Yet placed together, suddenly each seems questionable if not fanciful. The general lesson in all this is clear. *Just when we are most confident that we understand something, we do well to consider that there might be another, perhaps better, explanation.*

More specifically to the major point we are pursuing in this book, we shouldn't automatically assume that parents are to blame for things they perhaps could not have helped. Okay, let's assume we understand this. Well, what of it? What practical difference does such understanding make in our daily lives? Are we thereby any less likely either to accept unwarranted blame or take unjustified credit for our children's development?

A note from a parent begins: "Your book *Stranger in the Nest* gave me a much better understanding of how much my daughter's personality development depended on her biology. She seems to have a hostile personality, very much like her father's and my mother's. I wish you had asked me to read your book 20 years ago." But then she adds: "I'm still going to beat myself up because I didn't realize that by giving in to her and not working harder to civilize her, I have made it harder for her to learn self-control." What *is* it with us parents! Why do we have so much trouble appreciating evidence that could liberate us from the illusion that we control how things turn out?

Four hundred years ago philosopher Francis Bacon offered a pretty good answer. "For the mind of man is so far from being like a smooth . . . clear glass [but] rather like an enchanted glass, full of superstitions." These "superstitions"—call them misconceptions or errors of reasoning—come from three sources: human nature, social fashion, and cultural tradition.

By understanding all three, we can better appreciate what we can and cannot make happen with our children. If this sounds good then, with a respectful nod to the dear old philosopher, I suggest we begin with a brief look at our human nature.

Imagine I give you a deck of cards, each containing a single printed word. The sequence of cards reads as follows:

ABOUT WAS GOOD-LOOKING WAY AND TREATING MADE OF THAT A HIM THE QUIET YOUNGSTER NICE HE MANNERS A THEM GIRLS WILD GO WITH

You read the words, card by card, while trying to commit them to memory. Not an easy thing to do but still you try your best. I then shuffle the cards and ask you to put them back in their original order.

You do so, then pass the reordered deck to a second person who reads through the cards and likewise tries to commit the words to memory. The deck is shuffled and he is asked to put the cards back in the order he first read them. He does so, then passes the reordered deck to yet a third person.

This procedure is repeated from person to person. And what do we find after the deck of cards passes through, say 16 people?

HE WAS A YOUNGSTER NICE QUIET WITH MANNER GOOD-LOOKING AND A WAY OF TREATING THEM THAT MADE THE GIRLS GO WILD ABOUT HIM

Isn't that something? What a difference from the original! Strictly speaking, it's inaccurate. Well yes, but then it's so much more sensible and charming than the original. And telling, too, for it reveals a curious trait we all share: seeing things as better organized and more meaningful than they may actually be. Our bias is so natural, so automatic, we may even remember things that weren't there or never happened!

Do I exaggerate? Then consider another finding. Suppose the following words are spoken:

BED REST TIRED NAP SLUMBER YAWN DOZE DREAM

What will we remember? In time, we might come to believe that "sleep" was one of the words we heard. Remembering "sleep" makes perfect sense, given all those other sleep-related words. You might even want to argue that recalling "sleep" is a sign of good intelligence! Still, facts are facts, and the fact is "sleep" was not one of those spoken words, no matter how much we might insist that it was.

Such observations raise an interesting question: How do we handle evidence that contradicts our beliefs. How do we handle, for example, evidence that contradicts our belief that what we did or failed to do as parents explains why our child turned out a particular way? The answer is that we tend to ignore, discount, or forget such inconvenient evidence. Or maybe we see and remember such evidence as being more compatible with our belief than it really is.

In this are we not like those 16 people in the example above who turned a meaningless word jumble into "youngster nice quiet with manner good looking." Are we not like those 16 people in the example above who recalled "sleep"? It's all so natural and we are all susceptible. Trouble is, without even realizing it, we can wind up defending false and troublesome beliefs that do us and our children no good.

Perhaps you are still thinking I exaggerate. Then how else might we explain different eyewitness accounts, for example, about the assassination of Abraham Lincoln? One eyewitness declared that the killer had leaped fifteen feet. Another declared that he had shimmied down a flagpole. There was no flagpole at the scene.

How too can we explain different eyewitness accounts of the man who killed police officer J. D. Tippit shortly after supposedly killing president Kennedy? One witness said that Oswald was wearing black trousers and a light tan or gray Eisenhower windbreaker, and that his complexion was "pale as a ghost." Another said he was wearing light gray trousers and a brown jacket, and that his complexion was "ruddy." Both eyewitnesses spoke with much confidence and little hesitation, not unlike Neubauer's compulsively neat twins who spoke confidently of how their upbringing influenced their personality.

As with explanations, so it is with memory, which is easily fooled. In the laboratory, college students are asked to view a Disney ad suggesting that they once shook hands with Bugs Bunny during a childhood trip to Disneyland. When interviewed some time later, some students "remember" that indeed they had actually shaken hands with Bugs Bunny. Yet this could not have happened. Bugs Bunny, a Warner Brothers cartoon character, is never featured on any Walt Disney Company property.

Fact is, faulty remembering is something we all do, one time or another, especially when it comes to things we care about. We might remember things about our childhood or upbringing that never happened or happened a different way from what we imagine.

Usually faulty memory has little or no consequence except for the happy sense of having explained something to our satisfaction. However, it can have tragic consequences for emotional life and family relationships when parents are unjustly blamed by people who should know better.

To see how truly awful this can get, consider some findings from psychologist Steven Ceci's research on children that bear out the problem of parent blaming.

Little girls are given a "medical exam" that only includes measuring the wrist with a ribbon, putting a label on the stomach, and tickling the foot with a stick. Afterwards, they are asked about the exam, for instance, did the doctor touch their vagina? Initially, children usually answer negatively to such questions, for their memory is quite good. Yet some of them, even without suggestion or prodding, can change their story radically, as in this example.

A few days after the examination, a father gives an anatomically correct doll to his daughter and asks about the visit. "So what did he do?" At this point, his child describes how the doctor strangled her by wrapping the ribbon around her neck and pulling "real tight." Next she picks up the doll, lays it out, and places a stick between its legs to show how the doctor put a stick in her vagina. To emphasize the point, she bangs the stick with a hammer. Then she picks up the doll, flops it over, and looks between the legs to show how the doctor had looked into her "hiney." According to the investigators, about half the children in their studies make up such stories.

With such spectacular findings we see how personal stress and feverish imagination can drive adults to accuse a parent of sexual abuse during their childhood. In some cases the accusation might prove true, say by a sibling's testimony. In most cases, however, it has proven false, that is, when so-called recovered memories of traumatic experience prove to be neurotic fantasies.

False accusations have brought untold emotional pain and damage to parents, but also to parent-surrogates. Innocent child-care workers falsely identified as crazed child abusers have been publicly embarrassed, even prosecuted and jailed. In one such story, a parent-surrogate supposedly took all the children in her care to a special room. There she made them urinate and defecate on each other. She also had them smear peanut butter on each other and lick it off. As the story went, she stabbed them with knives and forks and had forced sexual intercourse with the boys.

Some people believed this flapdoodle. Never mind that there were no physical marks on the children or any residue of bodily products on the floor, furniture, or clothes. Never mind that there were no implements of torture, and no robots or hidden magic rooms.

Incredibly, the more bizarre the reports, the more that some people believed them. They must be true, so the argument went, for how could a child make up such stuff? No matter what all sober parents appreciate: that the mind of a child is quite inventive and readily suggestible. Strange, isn't it, how the impulse to blame can go ballistic when it comes to parents and parent-surrogates?

Such cases, while extreme, are nevertheless important, for they illustrate just how otherwise sensible adults, like little children, can wind up acting irrationally, even cruelly, in response to all sorts of wretched nonsense. As one psychologist said about ghost stories: If they are completely ridiculous, then people feel more comfortable. It's as if they don't bother to distinguish between the possible, the unlikely, and the truly preposterous.

Extreme cases illustrate something else as well, something we have been exploring throughout this book. It's easy to fall into the trap of blaming parents for all sorts of developments they could hardly have predicted or controlled. Some of our supposedly wisest experts have fallen into such a trap. So says psychiatrist

Torrey who places much blame on Americas's most famous baby doctor.

Benjamin Spock persuaded two generations of American mothers that nursing, weaning, tickling, playing, toilet training, and the like are not the innocent things they seem. Rather they are psychic minefields that determine a child's lifelong personality traits.

Unfortunately, this view sends a double message. On the one hand, Spock's *Baby and Child Care* says to parents: "Trust yourself—you know more than you think." On the other hand, it suggests that any misstep will have enduring, negative effects. Such thinking, says Torrey, has "made parenting much more difficult because of the generally accepted theory that—to exaggerate it a little bit—if you look at your child cross-eyed, your child will never be the same again."

Okay, Torrey may be exaggerating, yet only a little if we are to believe our best science. And his main point is well taken. If experts can fall into the trap of parent blaming, how much easier is it for the rest of us to do likewise. If we can believe in fantastic stories about magic rooms and the like, how much easier it is to believe we are responsible for all sorts of things that are actually out of our control. Yet how good to know this so that we might liberate ourselves from misunderstanding and guilt!

Indeed, we are all susceptible to faulty ways of seeing and remembering, more than we ever suspect. We can remember events quite differently from how they actually were—indeed, even the opposite of how they were. We may miss a point or get it right and then eventually lose it. If we expect to see something because of what we "know" or need to be true, we may not see what is in plain sight. We may even see things that aren't even there!

Seeing is believing, we say. Our eyes don't lie. Yet looking at the diagram on the next page, we see a white triangle. It's not there, yet we see it nonetheless.

The white triangle reminds us of what we all do: use bits of suggestive information to create something illusory in the mind's eye. So here's the interesting question. *How many illusory explanations do we embrace as gospel truth? And more to the point, how many involve ourselves as parents or as children?*

Imagine a troubled boy named Tommy. We might easily assume that Tommy's antisocial or suicidal behavior comes mostly from the way he was brought up. After all, seeing is believing. Yet what if that "seeing" is mostly an illusion, like the explanations offered by Neubauer's twins? Perhaps Tommy's behavior and the behavior of his parents stem mostly from their shared genetic tendencies. In that case, Tommy would have turned out quite similar growing up with any pair of normal parents.

We are convinced that our unhappiness comes from having been ignored or abused by a beloved parent. But again, what if this "seeing" too is mostly an illusion? Our sensitive temperament and faulty perceptions might have doomed us to unhappiness, regardless of our upbringing. It may even have contributed to an unhappy, unsatisfying upbringing.

It's reasonable to think so, given that our personality influences our upbringing at least as much as our upbringing influences our personality. As journalist Liza Mundy says about why some children wind up in day care:

Every woman returning from maternity leave discovers the secret truth: that the real, relentless trauma of separation from your child is offset, if only a tiny bit, by the luxury of being able to . . . order a cup of coffee! And drink it! Just sit there and drink it! All of which prompted, for me, a question about the child-care study . . . that found that 17 percent of children in child care tend to behave aggressively, while the same is true of only 6 percent of children cared for by mothers.

113

No one knows what this signifies; the study's own researchers disagree over whether it suggests moms should stay home or child care should be made better . . . . But what struck me was that the only question being asked was whether child care . . . causes aggression in kids, and if so how. Privately, I began nursing another hypothesis: Could it be that aggressive children cause their mothers to work?

So again, when we hear something like, "No wonder little Billy is so troubled, just look at his parents," again I suggest we at least consider that alternative possibility. "No wonder his parents are so troubled, just look at little Billy."

Yet there's still another possibility that is both more subtle and as likely to be true. *Little Billy and his parents share genetic tendencies,* for instance, to be willful and demanding. If so, then little Billy might have turned out to be difficult even if raised by loving adoptive parents. Of course, we can never know, when it comes to Billy. Still, it *is* worth considering, if only to be fair.

We can apply this genetic approach to all kinds of serious questions about family life—divorce, for instance. Whatever the current rate of divorce, some people will always be at higher risk than others. Why? Is it something about their upbringing or is it having experienced a family breakdown?

Children of divorced parents no doubt have a rough time. While most wind up doing well, some remain troubled with feelings of anxiety, alienation, resentment, depression and fantasies of abandonment. Some are disposed to sexual promiscuity, crime, alcohol and drug abuse—even suicide. They have relatively poor social adjustment at school, lower academic achievement, and a high risk of falling below the poverty line. Eventually, they may have troubled marriages, many ending in divorce.

Who are these children who seem less able than others to bounce back from the trauma of broken family life? In the conventional view they are, like all children, victims of social forces. The little diagram below shows this with an arrow going from parents to children:

Our diagram suggests one obvious solution to the problem of such troubled children. Lower the divorce rate. But how do you accomplish this when a do-your-own-thing pop culture so readily

Parents   ⟶   Children
(divorce)   (troubled)

tolerates and even encourages divorce?

All right, let's say we really can get the divorce rate lower. Perhaps getting parents to remain together will help lower the risk of divorce in the next generation. Still, some children are more likely than others to become a divorced parent, whatever the current divorce rate and however much we get that rate down. Why? Who are these high-risk children who seem to defy our ready explanations?

Before venturing an answer, let's consider how people who divorce, especially more than once, might differ from those who don't. Such people will tend to be, for instance, more impulsive, demanding, irresponsible, or self-centered. Now, we've seen that such traits are strongly influenced by genes. So there's really no surprise that over 50 percent of all influences that increase the risk of divorce are the genetic kind.

Most likely, the children of divorced parents will have inherited more than their fair share of such influences. Such shared heredity could partially explain why the parent's conflict becomes so destructive. It could also explain why the child's troubles are so deep and lasting, as illustrated here.

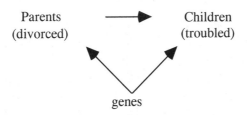

Parents   ⟶   Children
(divorced)   (troubled)

genes

Our new diagram doesn't indicate which is the stronger influence, the social kind from parents to children or the genetic kind they both share. Well, what if the genetic kind proved to be the stronger? Consider a few facts.

115

Divorce runs in families. Our chance of divorcing is relatively high if our parents divorced. It's even higher if both our and our spouse's parents divorced. Yet the reason seems to be genetic more than social, assuming we believe what twin studies are telling us. Moreover, this could explain something interesting about the children of divorced parents. They are more likely than other children to be seriously troubled, not just during a family breakup but long before, during early childhood, and long after, during adolescence and beyond.

Well, what if the genetic factor indeed proved to be the stronger influence? In that case, efforts to prevent divorce by lessening parental conflict might not be as effective as we would like. We'd have a harder time preventing troubled children from becoming troubled adults with a high risk of divorce. This conclusion, like so many other things we've explored, may seem to contradict conventional wisdom. Nevertheless, it does make sense if, as our best evidence suggests, divorce is as much a biological fact as a social fact of family life.

All this genetic business is easy enough to understand when we bother to reflect. Yet it's just as easy to forget when the wayward behavior of our child cries out for ready explanation. Ready explanations come from things we can see and/or imagine. Family life is so multicolored, so tangible while genetic influence is so pale and abstract. The one touches us in a personal way that the other cannot.

When Uncle George is acting crazy and scaring the hell out of Aunt Martha and the kids, we want sensible reasons that appeal to our intuition and experience. We don't want a bunch of statistical facts or genetic theory, for even if we understand them in general, we don't *feel* them in situations involving real children.

It's a fact of human nature and social life. Even true, easily understood facts are easily forgotten or ignored in the heat of the moment. Some of us get all worked up by seeing a lottery winner on TV or a slot-machine winner in the casino. Enthralled by intox-

116

icating images of big winnings, we imagine we can be a winner, though the odds are we can't. Even knowing the odds, we still act as if the rules of the game don't apply to us.

Someone must win big, we think, but who? Cold-blooded statistics say it won't be us even as our hot-blooded fantasies say it *will*. Well, the odds of winning big with a lottery ticket are actually less than the odds of being hit by an airplane falling out of the sky. A witty person once said that our chance of winning $10 million by purchasing a lottery ticket is about as good as our chance of getting money by standing in front of an ATM machine and braying like a donkey.

Statistics are cold; they don't bleed. Even a good statistic won't touch us beyond a few moments like a memorable story, especially a scary one about a person.

Speaking about recent school shootings in the San Diego area, criminologist Gary Kleck offered this observation. Scary-world imagery promoted by the media gives the false impression that things are going from bad to worse, when just the opposite may be closer to the truth. "One would scarcely guess from the recent heated public discussion that violence, gun violence, mass murder and school violence have all dramatically declined in recent years, or that the juvenile homicide rate has dropped by 58% since 1991."

It's just human nature that "hot" stories trump cold statistics. We just can't appreciate remote statistical facts in the face of personal testimony and strong emotion. Unfortunately, it's a weakness that can sometimes wind up hurting innocent people, as beautifully illustrated by an extraordinary story told by criminologist Lawrence Sherman.

"On Oct. 30, 1985, Sylvia Seegrist walked into the Springfield Mall in suburban Philadelphia and started to shoot at random with a .22 caliber semi-automatic rifle. Her bullets hit 10 people, killing three of them. She was later ruled criminally insane." To make sense of this event, a rational juror needs an answer to this key question: How likely is a Seegrist-type event?

117

Seegrist had apparently made threats, yet a study of 110 cases involving threats found that none had led to serious injury, let alone murder. Threats are usually just talk. As Sherman says, "From 1976 to 1984, there was only about one crime a year similar to this one in the entire U.S.: simultaneous murder of three or more people by a stranger, not for monetary gain, using a gun. Only seven people a year, on average die from such an offense. Lightning strikes some 80 people dead each year, and auto accidents kill 50,000. The odds of a plaintiff dying in a mass murder were about 1 in 30 million."

Then how about in the Seegrist crime? "The annual odds . . . of Ms. Seegrist committing the crime were only 1 in 156 million, without considering her sex. The prior rate of such crimes by women nationwide was zero. There also had been no prior documented mass murder in a shopping center." The Seegrist crime was thus essentially unpredictable.

Apparently unimpressed by the logic of such statistics, a jury found the mall to be negligent!

Outrageous, yes, but I ask you. *What's the difference between blaming authorities for a crazy woman's unpredictable rampage in a mall and blaming parents for a crazy adolescent's unpredictable rampage in a high school?* Perhaps we might have—perhaps we should have—recognized the signs of mental illness in both the woman and the adolescent. Even so, what could we have done about it?

Let's say we discover that adolescent murderers show signs of emotional disturbance. These might include depression and social withdrawal because of bullying. Perhaps there are angry e-mails, threatening comments, or a preoccupation with weapons or pornography. Nevertheless, the statistics are clear and their implication well worth considering. Almost no adolescent displaying such signs ever murders anyone. Remember what was found in the Sylvia Seegrist case? Seegrist had apparently made threats. Yet a study of 110 cases involving threats found that none had led to serious injury, let alone murder.

Once again, please understand that absolutely nothing in these observations lets irresponsible parents of troubled adolescents off the hook of social condemnation. But what about the rest of us parents, what should we do with our troubled adolescents? Would restricting, docking, punishing, or moralizing do any good? Short of locking up every one of them, how could we ever prevent the occasional disaster like the massacre at Columbine High? Indeed, how could we if the tragic effects of mental illness heightened by peer pressure and popular culture are mostly beyond a parent's control? It's a question we must ask if only in the interest of fairness to parents.

Rare events like the Seegrist and Columbine killings forcefully remind us of something we hardly ever consider unless compelled by bad things that seem to happen out of the blue. *There's a random element in our lives.* Call it luck, good luck or bad. Call it the roll of genetic and environmental "dice." Call it what you will, some things just happen for "no good reason," like having a genius or autistic child.

The random element is one reason why we can count on things being different the next time. It's a reason why our other children most likely *won't* be geniuses or autistic. It's a reason why the children of alcoholics, schizophrenics, or diabetics, despite their increased risk, are *not* likely to succumb to a mental illness. Appreciating all this means being more realistic, and for some of us less guilty, about our supposed influence.

All we've explored in this chapter reminds us of something easily forgotten in the heat of the moment. A false but compelling idea can easily swamp a true but less compelling one. Walking under an unoccupied ladder will not cause harm. Sure, we say, we know that. Yet faced with a real ladder, some of us would never do so under any circumstances.

After the bowling ball has left our hand, what do some of us do? We might arch our back and flail our arms. Such frantic movement cannot possibly influence the ball's trajectory. Yes, we know that. Still, in the heat of the moment, who's really thinking? It just feels right to flail, and never mind the facts; we go with our "flow."

Our child's biology greatly limits our influence. Well yes, we know that too, if only from the differences we see in our children right from the beginning, and yes, after reading a book like this. Yet what difference does our understanding make in the way we go about parenting? Are we thereby less apprehensive, less demanding, less guilt-ridden, or less self-congratulatory? And what difference does it make in our enthusiasm for child-rearing books that downplay biology? Perhaps recalling that our second child was always so different from the first would challenge our belief in our power to mold our children. Yet as journalist Steve Sailer once noted, "Child-rearing books hush this up because their market is first-time parents."

It's why I suggest a simple rule of thumb. Always treat opinion and advice offered by experts as you would treat "great deals" offered by telemarketers: with extreme caution if not outright skepticism. For a while the experts may seem wise, yet prove otherwise.

Chapter 10
Reflections of Society

Years ago during a eulogy at an American funeral, a British fellow advised the bereaved husband to "keep his pecker up." What could he have been thinking?! Well, it seems that in England, keeping your pecker up can mean having courage in the face of adversity.

Clearly, even well-intentioned people who speak the same language can easily misinterpret one another. Likewise for us and our children, and for us and the world outside the family. Our social world is awash in misunderstandings and misinformation about parental influence and responsibility.

Consider how easily we are misled especially when fashionable views or scientific findings presented by the media are couched in images and words that seduce and confuse. We hear, for example, that Brand X is "unsurpassed." Should we be impressed? Not if we recognize that this phrase means only that no other brand is better. All of them including Brand X might be equally mediocre. For all we know, they all might be equally ineffective!

They tell us that Brand X is "new and improved," but improved from what and by how much? Let's say the old version was 50 percent effective, whatever that means. Then a 60-percent effective "new and improved" version isn't so impressive.

An ad says: "Nine out of 10 doctors recommend Brand X." Sounds impressive, but wait. What we aren't told is that doctors see no difference between Brands X, Y, and Z. When asked, most say, "Sure, I recommend Brand X, just as I recommend Brands Y and Z." Of course, the ad leaves out the Y and Z part!

Imprecise language can also obscure the truth, as with these amusing headlines: "Iraqi Head Seeks Arms," "Prostitutes Appeal to Pope," "Teacher Strikes Idle Kids," "Miners Refuse to Work after Death," "Teachers Request More Time For Sex," and my favorite: "Kids Make Nutritious Snacks."

If these examples aren't sufficiently impressive, consider one more example, this one in the form of an apparently outrageous statement. "Woman without her man would be a savage." Before you take issue with me or with that sentence, let's add a little punctuation. "Woman, without her, man would be a savage." Now I ask, if a "little thing" like punctuation can so mislead, how many other imprecise "little things" likewise mislead us, and how often? Answer: Many and quite often.

Experts tell us that poor parenting "plays a role" in mental illness X, but wait. Does "plays a role" mean that poor parenting is a major cause of illness X? After all, one could say about even a trivial influence that it "plays a role." Imagine that, out of all the influences on trait X, the parenting kind amounted to just 10 percent while the genetic kind amounted to 90 percent. You could still say that genes and parenting both play a role. But how would that be a fair indication of what's going on? How would that illuminate the key causes of trait X? In my view, we are poorly served by vague words like "plays a role," for they are mostly empty and often misleading.

It's not just imprecise language but inaccurate messages that cloud the truth. Mathematician John Paulos describes a newspaper story about the suicide of 28 teens who had often played the game Dungeons and Dragons. The article suggested that the 28 had become obsessed with the game and lost contact with reality. Apparently, we parents should discourage our teens from playing such a dangerous game.

It seems like an obvious conclusion, doesn't it? After all, seeing is believing. But is it a smart conclusion? Twenty-eight suicides do seem like a lot, but is it so? I mean, compared to what?

Don't we need to know how many teens *usually* commit suicide, for whatever reason?

Well, we do know. Of every 3 million teens, about 360 commit suicide each year. Yet, for the 3 million teens who played Dungeons and Dragons, the number was just 28! Suddenly, that number seems relatively small. Now it seems we parents should *encourage* our teens to play such a wonderful game!

Then again, maybe not, for there's another possibility. Perhaps what matters most is neither the game nor the parents but the kind of teen who seeks out and enjoys playing such games. Perhaps such teens have a greater zest for life or maybe a greater fear of death. Either way, encouraging or discouraging play won't alter the risk of suicide because it can't change personalities that seek out the game.

No doubt about it. It's not just what we see that may matter most, but what we *don't* see. Likewise, it's not just what we are told that may matter most, but what we *aren't* told. Imagine, while reading a newspaper account of a study on guns and crime, we come across this finding: 74 percent of boys who illegally possessed guns committed street crimes, compared with 24 percent of boys who had no guns. What does this finding suggest about guns?

Before you answer, consider another finding left out of the article: Only 14 percent of boys who owned a gun *legally*, that is, with their parents' consent, committed street crimes. Moreover, *none* of them committed any sort of gun crime. This finding would surely suggest something rather different about guns than so-called conventional wisdom would have us believe.

Moral of the story: As with games and guns, so it is with parenting and child development. Without having all the relevant information—without having an open mind and some healthy skepticism—we can easily slip from seductive half-truths to whole-cloth falsehoods.

Professor Robert Hutchins once wrote about a mess sergeant who asks a private why he keeps demanding more coffee. "You like coffee, don't you?" "Yes," replies the private, "*good* coffee. That's why I am willing to go through so much hot water to get some." Likewise, we parents must be willing to go through many "hot" stories to get to something true and useful.

One "hot" claim was that exposure to classical music can make two-year-olds grow up smarter and healthier. Enchanted with this notion of a "Mozart effect," a governor of Georgia once signed a bill to send every new Georgia newborn home from the hospital with a Mozart CD. Good idea?

No doubt, Mozart's music is wonderful, but that's not the question parents want answered. Rather, they want to know if frequent exposure to Mozart's music during early childhood can really help their children grow up smarter and healthier? Not likely, and here's why.

The initial finding of a boost in "intelligence" from exposure to Mozart's music was based on a study of a few college students, not children. These students took a paper-folding test, not an intelligence test. The effect, whatever it was, lasted for only a few minutes, not longer. Most important, attempts to duplicate the initial finding have failed.

One observer commented sarcastically, "No one has told the publishers, for there are seminars on TV, book signings at Borders, window displays of CDs and books of Mozart for babies and any number of books still being published etc. People seem to think there is a lot of money to be made with this schtick." Another observer concluded sadly: "Exaggerated and false claims about music have become so commonplace that it is probably a waste of time to try to correct them."

Let's imagine that music during the "formative years" really does boost brain activity and therefore reading or math performance. Even so, any effect might be weak or short-lasting. I therefore doubt it would justify the hoopla, cost, effort, and finally the disappointment. In my view, children are as likely to become more intelligent by hearing Mozart as they are to become more antisocial by eating bread. What about bread eating is bad for kids? Here's what one clever fellow reported.

More than 98 percent of convicted felons are bread users. Half of all children who grow up in bread-consuming households score below average on standardized tests.

In the 18th century, when virtually all bread was baked in the home, the average life expectancy was less than 50 years. Infant mortality rates were terribly high. Many women died in childbirth and diseases, such as typhoid, yellow fever, and influenza ravaged whole nations. Wait, there's more.

Over 90 percent of violent crimes are committed within 24 hours of eating bread. Bread has been proven to be addictive. Subjects deprived of bread and given only water to eat beg for bread after as little as two days. Bread is often a "gateway" food, leading the user to "harder" items, such as butter, jelly, peanut butter, and even cold cuts.

Such witty piffle does nevertheless help make a serious point. All the statistical babbling about parenting is no more useful than those "statistics" on bread eating. No wonder we parents are so easily misled by bogus information dressed up in statistics. No wonder we so readily accept not just blame for what we supposedly did wrong but advice on what we should do to make things right. As it has been said: "There are lies, damned lies, and statistics."—good to remember, if we parents are to remain properly vigilant.

Scanning the papers and magazines, we find the latest discovered connection between the rearing environment and its influence on children. "Talking to an infant increases the number of words she will recognize and eventually come to understand . . . ." This sentence, which appeared in a local paper, sounds convincing enough. It makes us want to rush cribside and start yacking. Good idea?

Fact is, there's no good evidence that talking more to an infant than we normally do has *any* lasting beneficial effect. Even if there were a significant effect, it might prove rather small. So until we know otherwise, I suggest we save the extra yacking and give our kids more hugs and kisses. Even if these proved not to make them brighter or even happier adults, so what? It will make everyone feel good and help engender fond memories and strengthen family ties, which is more than enough, don't you think?

Now let's consider a few more illustrative examples—we are inundated with these sorts of things all the time in the papers and magazines and on TV talk shows—of how the rearing environment supposedly has a major influence.

- ". . . being at home during those early years or being employed during those years are both good choices . . . *can result in* healthy, well-developed children."

- "Low warmth [little affection] accompanied by high punishment *led* to an average decrease of 12 IQ points . . . ."

- "Inconsistent parenting leads the child to conclude that behaving well doesn't get results."

- "Children do worse on developmental tests if their mothers are depressed, but a mother's depression *does less damage* if the family is well off financially . . . ."

- "Household rituals [such as gathering for meals] *might help* children fare better emotionally in the face of disruptive problems including alcoholism . . . ."

- " . . . paddling only *leads* to further misbehavior . . . ."

Such familiar statements, with those emphasized words, seem to say a lot about what causes what. Yet each may be only partly true or even mostly false. Some of them may be little more than an expert opinion. Granted, such opinion may rest on research. Yet we've seen how often research findings can be ambiguous when they support more than one idea about parenting and child development.

My favorite example of such ambiguity comes from an expert who once declared Johnny Carson to be "single-handedly responsible for Americans' lousy sex lives. People are watching him instead of having sex." Maybe for some this was true. For others, the reverse was surely true. Lousy sex lives were creating excuses to watch Johnny.

So there it is: an expert offering only one of two possible opinions on some observation, this one about TV watching. Well, it happens all the time. Worse, we can easily be misled. Take, for example, a commonly held opinion that goes like this: "Mothers who are overly strict and punitive and who tend not to rely on reason or consistent rules will likely impede their children's [positive social] development."

This opinion has the ring of truth. It seems all the more reasonable, as it is based on a solid finding. Compared to other boys, the sons of such tough mothers are much less able to appreciate another person's suffering. "These boys may have experienced more emotional, and possibly physical, pain in their maternal relationships than had the other children."

Yet the key question is hardly ever asked, so let's ask it. Is such harsh parenting really *the main cause* of emotional problems

Harsh Parenting   ⟶   Antisocial Sons

that last a lifetime, as diagrammed here?

Given everything we've talked about, isn't it likely that the genetic reasons for a parent's harsh behavior could also promote a child's problem traits? In short, what if this second diagram is closer to the truth?

This second diagram suggests two big possibilities. One is that both our parenting and our children's development are related in

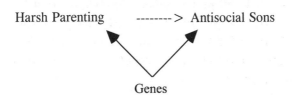

Harsh Parenting   --------> Antisocial Sons

Genes

127

part because of our shared genes. The dark arrows make that clear enough. The other possibility is that this shared genetic influence is even stronger than our own parenting influence. What else could explain why identical twins reared apart are so much more alike than even fraternal twins reared together?

Where genetic influence is relatively strong, statements such as those listed above can be terribly misleading about parents' responsibility for the ways their children turn out. Naturally, it's not something we'd want to hear when the mothers in question are irresponsible or abusive. Our natural instinct is to condemn and blame them. Yet ignoring a possible genetic influence can lead us into the trap of confusing responsibility for bad parenting and responsibility for bad outcomes.

Such confusion is less likely if we keep in mind that second diagram and two obvious facts of life. Good outcomes sometimes follow bad parenting, while bad outcomes sometimes follow good parenting. These facts don't mean that the quality of our parenting doesn't matter. Of course it matters. For some things it matters a lot. It's just that for other things, it matters little or hardly at all.

All I'm suggesting here is that we keep in mind that good old proverb, "Look before you leap," not just before buying a car or appliance but also before buying into some supposedly expert opinion about our parenting and our child's development.

We need to be smarter consumers of evidence because we know how very misleading evidence can be. Yet we need not be fooled, if only we appreciate how often easy answers may be false. We've seen this with easy answers to questions about personality, alcoholism, child abuse, and homosexuality. It's the same with easy answers to questions about all sorts of traits, including IQ.

The moral of this story is clear. *Explanations for our parenting and our child's development are easy to come by. Some may prove mostly true, others mostly false. Until then, we parents will do well to keep both an open mind and a skeptical eye lest we rush unhappily to judgment.*

We've seen how easy it is to assume social influence in findings that just as well suggest genetic influence. And we've seen how this can lead us astray when it comes to understanding why our children turn out the way they do. Let me suggest another pitfall, starting with this typical report of a finding.

Parents take heed. Your adolescent son or daughter is likely to do as you do—especially when it comes to adopting risky health behaviors, such as cigarette smoking . . . A new study of 330 adolescents and their parents found that parents who smoked cigarettes, drank excessive amounts of alcohol, led sedentary lifestyles, consumed poor diets, or got inadequate sleep were more likely to have adolescent children with the same habits and/or behaviors than were parents who did not indulge in such risky health behaviors.

According to the lead investigator, "Adolescents who are constantly exposed to parents' health-risk behavior, such as poor eating habits, smoking and drinking will tend to emulate their parents' behavior." This notion of emulation is so appealing. Who can resist?

Yet consider the key question. Why *don't* most children emulate their parents? After all, many heavy smokers were brought up by non-smoker parents. Why no emulation? Likewise, many non-smokers have heavy-smoker parents. Again, why no emulation? If we can't explain these apparent "exceptions" to the rule, shouldn't we at least question the rule? I say we should.

When I was growing up, many people smoked cigarettes. Matinee idols did, many parents did, including my mother. All us kids "smoked" candy cigarettes at one time or another. It made us feel more adult. When older, some of us experimented with real ones, yet few became serious smokers. I tried it a few times but found it distasteful.

Moral of the cigarette-smoking story: *Children do what they need to do, imitating this, practicing that, before moving on to other things. It's the play and work of being a kid. It's children learning in their own way on their own terms to their own ends.*

"Children have never been very good at listening to their elders," says author James Baldwin, "but they have never failed to imitate them." Imitation may delight us and flatter us too. Yet it may just as well mislead us when it proves to be other than it seems.

On the way to preschool, the physician had left her stethoscope on the car seat. Her little four-year-old daughter picked it up and began playing with it. "Be still, my heart," thought the mother, "my daughter wants to follow in my footsteps!" Then the child spoke into the instrument, "Welcome to McDonald's. May I take your order?"

Imitation need not mean emulation in any deep or lasting sense. For years, my son imitated Superman. Yet none of this was the kind of imitation that means true emulation. Jason certainly had no interest in jumping out windows or fighting for justice and the American way. Does imitating a parent have any more lasting effect on a child's personality than imitating a super hero? Does imitation really explain why a child follows in a parent's footsteps? I doubt it.

To see better why I say so, consider a headline that reads: "Children don't follow parent's alcohol habits." Well, that sounds about right, but wait. According to the article:

Though many believe the children of heavy drinkers will follow their parents down the road to excessive alcohol consumption, a [new] study refutes this. Children of heavy drinkers did not drink as much as their parents while children of teetotalers tended to drink . . . . Children [emulated] their parents' drinking habits only in the middle range.

So there it is, only so-called middle-range children respond to social influence by emulating or rejecting their parents' behavior. That's what the article says, and that too seems reasonable enough to anyone not familiar with all we have been exploring. But once again, it pays to ask: Is it really so? Are so-called middle-range children, unlike other children, really emulating or rejecting their parents' behavior? Probably not or at least not much, and here are three good reasons.

First reason: The genetic element in family life. The alcoholism rate for the close relatives of male alcoholics is perhaps four times higher than normal. More to the point, this high rate is found even for men born to alcoholics but adoptively reared by normal parents. Twin studies even suggest that, at least for men, genetic influence may be as much as 60 percent of all influences.

And of the remaining 40 percent, or "environmental" influences, how much comes from parents? Well, we can't be sure. For all anyone knows, risk for alcoholism may have more to do with prenatal life than with how a person was brought up.

Second reason: The random element in family life. Alcoholism does tend to run in some families more than in others. Yet most members of such families don't abuse alcohol, and most children raised by alcoholic parents don't become alcoholics. Likewise with the children of diabetics or schizophrenics: Most won't ever succumb to these disorders. The reason is partly chance, the much lower chance that the genetic and environmental factors behind a parent's illness will occur in a child.

Third reason: The illusory element in family life. Let's say the development of alcohol dependence has little to do with a parent's personal habits or a child's apparent emulation. Can it be likewise for many other developments involving our children's personality, intelligence, mental health, and character?

Apparently it can, given all that we've explored in this book. It means that some of our influence is more illusory than real. Naturally, all of it may seem real because we control so much of what our children *do*. Yet some of it isn't real because we control so little of what our children are.

Failure to appreciate the genetic, random, and illusory elements in our lives makes us more likely to embrace weak explanations while ignoring strong ones. Buyer beware. As I've said, when it comes to hot findings and fashionable opinions about how to raise our children—a healthy dose of skepticism is the smart way to go.

Chapter 11
Reflections of Culture

As it is with fashionable ideas and personal experience, so it is with cultural traditions. Both can mislead us about our influence as parents. Love conquers all, we say. We look at newborns and see educational possibilities, not inborn potentials. We naturally assume that anything is possible with love, guidance, and opportunity. Yet so much of what we've seen suggests rather that anything is *not* possible.

Still, with any large group of families there will always be success stories, say with troubled or handicapped children. Such stories naturally strengthen our belief that anything is possible. Of course, with some child somewhere, some things will be possible. But what about with a particular child—ours, for instance? Ask the parents of a severely hyperactive, antisocial, mentally retarded, or autistic child—ask just the parents of an average child—if anything is possible.

Granted all sorts of things are possible, but not anything and not nearly as much as anecdotes or personal experience may suggest. Ignoring that fact of life, we tend to blame even devoted parents for not having loved enough or tried hard enough, which in many cases is unrealistic as well as unfair.

Still, we have mixed feelings about inborn influences that limit what we can accomplish. As a parent of two adopted children wrote to me:

All parents are concerned about the welfare of their children and wonder how their behavior and parenting skills will affect their children. We sometimes think that we can completely control what our children do. The idea that this is not true can be both frightening and freeing. Frightening because we want to protect our children. Freeing because it takes away some of the guilt when something bad happens.

Yes we have mixed feelings about inborn influences, especially the genetic kind. So maybe we ignore or deny it. Maybe we accept it, but with little enthusiasm. Or, because we see it in our children's behavior as well as their faces, just maybe we simply accept it with good humor.

An old man is sitting on a park bench, feeding the pigeons. A young man of about 20, with hair dyed blue, yellow, green, and red, sits down next to him. The old man stares and the young man says, "Why are you staring? Haven't you done anything wild when you were young?" "Yes," replied the old man. "Twenty years ago I got drunk and had sex with a parrot, so I was just wondering if you were my child."

* * *

Evidence of biological influence on our children and ourselves challenges all sorts of beliefs. It surely challenges the traditional idea that "all men are created equal." Indeed all of us are equal yet we are not the same.

We are equal in the legal or spiritual sense yet not in the psychological sense. It's evident to unbiased common sense and in all we've explored, especially the genetic reasons for sibling differences in temperament, talent, IQ, personality, character, and mental health. It's certainly evident to any thoughtful parent with more than one child!

Still, it may seem unfair that our children don't start out with a level playing field. Yet where is it written that life is fair? What's fair about adversity striking individuals willy-nilly? What's fair about good guys dying young or bad guys getting the gals and the gold?

Once again, it seems to me, Ecclesiastes says it best. "The race is not [necessarily] to the swift, nor the battle to the strong, neither yet bread to the wise, nor yet riches to men of understanding, nor yet favor to men of skill; but time and chance happeneth to them all."

The seeming injustice of it all may partly explain the sometimes passionate yet misguided denial that our genes make us different from each other in important ways, "bad" ways as well as "good." Recall, for illustration, two impressive things suggesting why we differ in our vulnerability to alcoholism.

One is the alcoholism rate for the close relatives of male alcoholics, which is perhaps four times higher than normal. This high rate is found even for men born to alcoholics but reared by normal adoptive parents. The other is genetic influence, which may be as much as 60 percent of all the influences that put men at risk for becoming alcoholics.

Such evidence surely challenges any great confidence about alcoholism being mostly a matter of children emulating parents, even alcoholic parents. Yet incredibly, we hear from a so-called expert that the best predictors of alcoholism aren't biological at all! Rather, he says, they are "psychological factors," such as whom you hang out with or whether you have a job.

Sure, but why pretend that such psychological factors don't reflect strong genetic influence when our best evidence says they do? Calling the whole genetic argument misguided and unjustified may make some hearts go pitter-patter. Yet what benefit do we get if good feelings come at the cost of truth obscured or denied?

An otherwise sober scientist proclaims: "There is not one jot or tittle of evidence of any genetic basis for any behavioral trait, except schizophrenia—whether it be intelligence or nastiness or aggressiveness." What an incredible comment, given all we now know about genetic influence in all areas of our lives.

A contemporary philosopher offers an even more astonishing, truly hideous comment. "If there is a gene that predisposes for dyslexia, or violence—or musical genius or homosexuality—*it might be better for us to be kept in the dark about such things.*"

What?! Kept in the dark? By whom and how do they get to decide what to keep from the rest of us? Who makes them privileged gatekeepers of forbidden knowledge? I don't know about you, but I am alarmed by such false philanthropy.

It's what I felt when an editor once wrote me the following: "You yourself say that your thesis doesn't in any way let parents off the hook of good parenting, so parents will continue to buy the books that help them be better parents. *To the extent that parents are deluding themselves, it might be a necessary delusion.*"

What this editor, like that philosopher, seems to be saying is this: Parents who read books on parenting and child development are nevertheless too dumb or fragile to handle certain facts of child development and family life. Better to keep them protected from the truth. If I believed that nonsense, I would never have written this book.

No doubt, the idea of genetic influence can trouble us. It seems to deny our ability to change ourselves and our children for the better, which troubles optimistic people. It seems to deny the sanctity of the individual, which troubles religious people. It seems to deny a person's responsibility for his own behavior, which can offend conservatives. It suggests that any difference between groups, say in intelligence or criminal behavior, can't be remedied however heroic the effort, which can offend liberals. Finally, it seems to deny that parents are in control, which troubles anyone who believes that we should credit good parents for their child's achievement, but blame awful parents for their child's failures.

Yet what if such ideas are somewhat misguided or even way off the mark? For example, the idea that we are governed by genetic influence seems to deny our dignity as individuals with "free will." That troubles us. Okay, but why don't we feel the same about being governed by social influence? Doesn't being a "product of our environment" likewise deny our dignity and "free will"?

Of course in some ways we are products of our environment, but where is the dignity in that? As science writer Matt Ridley asks: "If you're going to be pushed around, would you rather be pushed around by your environment, which is not you, or by your genes, which in some sense is who you are?" It's a good question well worth pondering.

Yes, an unusually strong dose of genetic influence may sometimes overwhelm a person, as with evil or genius or mental illness. Yet it need not be so, and normally it isn't so. When we speak of genetic influence, we usually mean statistics—averages—not individuals. For any one person, our child, for instance, its influence on a trait can be strong or weak or anything in between.

All this is true, but there's a larger point. *Genetic influence normally doesn't rule out personal responsibility or social influence. It doesn't get parents off the hook of social condemnation when it comes to a child's attitudes and behavior. It merely makes a parent's job more challenging.*

After reading what I just said in a draft of this book, a mother of two pre-teens offered the following comment.

You seem to be saying that parents need to look at their children. They need to realize that with this trait I can have some influence, with that one less influence. With some I may have no influence at all. So, as a mother, I want to provide a "best-odds" environment for my children.

Bingo! We parents really do have less long-term influence than we imagine. Moreover, we've seen the evidence and let's say we are convinced, but so what? We are no less responsible for doing the best job we can. Responsible parenting is all about *trying* to promote civilized behavior and positive potentials. It is not necessarily about succeeding.

So again, the biological view we've been exploring doesn't deny the obvious, that our parenting is essential and that good parenting is better than bad parenting. Rather, that biological view makes clear why we parents must do all we can and hope for the best. It makes clear why there can be no guarantees: why we and our children may not live happily ever after—yet also why we may.

Chapter 12
Beyond Reflections

A hundred years ago, many poor Americans suffered from a nasty disease called pellagra. They suffered from diarrhea, dermatitis, running sores, vomiting, dizziness, impaired reasoning, agitation, and depression. Medical experts insisted that poor sanitation was the culprit. Yet people with poor sanitation also had poor nutrition. So which one was the true culprit?

Physician Joseph Goldberger believed it was poor nutrition, not poor sanitation. To prove his maverick theory, he didn't just argue the point. Rather, he put healthy people on a high carbohydrate, low protein diet. They soon developed pellagra, just as he had predicted. (The deeper cause was a lack of niacin, one of the B vitamins, a fact discovered eight years after Goldberger died.)

Goldberger didn't stop there. He then set out to disprove the idea that the culprit was poor sanitary conditions. Incredibly, he injected himself with the blood of pellagra victims. He ate their nose secretions. He ate scrapings from their sores. He even ate little pellagra balls made of flour mixed with their urine and feces! The result was no pellagra, again as he had predicted.

Was Goldberger nuts? Maybe a little. Okay, more than a little! Yet he was passionately clear-eyed about one important thing. Only through a lively competition of testable ideas can we ever discover the truth. With twin and adoption studies, for instance, we can discover if conventional wisdom is on or off the mark. Without it, we fail to recognize how our own perspective—what we are biased to see, feel, and think—may be half a truth or even no truth at all.

Looking at the drawing below, you probably see a cake pan with a cake missing just one piece. Yet turn the page upside down

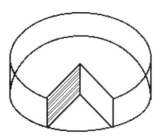

and I'll bet you now see just a single piece of cake. In the one view, the cake is mostly there. In the other, it mostly isn't there.

Likewise with evidence about human behavior. Looked at one way, it seems to favor social explanation. Looked at another way, it seems to favor biological explanation. Some of us embrace the one, some embrace the other. Each side may be mostly right about some aspect of a problem yet wrong about other aspects.

Often we don't make clear what aspect we are talking about. So we wind up taking sides and talking past each other. Each side may even question the other's competence or assume that the other is acting in bad faith.

This can easily happen with hot topics like homosexuality, suicide, or child abuse, especially when we ignore findings from adoption studies and new knowledge about prenatal life that give us insights we never had before. So how might we find out the truth? To see how, consider for illustration one kind of destructive behavior that concerns all of us.

Why do some children, when grown up, abuse their own children? To get an answer, we typically adopt the *abuser's perspective* by looking back to his childhood. No surprise, many child abusers, 40 percent or more, say they were abused during their childhood. From this, conventional wisdom says abusive parenting is a major cause of child abuse.

138

Seems reasonable, but wait. Let's now adopt the *abused child's perspective.* Follow abused children forward into adulthood and what do we find? Relatively few such children—maybe 25 percent—become child-abuser parents. Our change in perspective makes it seem less clear that bad rearing is a major cause of child abuse. But if it isn't a major cause, what is?

A great way to find out, we have seen, is with adoptive children. Unlike other children, adoptive children have two sets of parents: biological parents they've never known and adoptive parents they've known all their lives. From the one set, they get their genetic influences. From the other set, they get their parenting influences. With adoptive children we could therefore find out which kind of influence is the stronger.

So let's imagine we do such a study, say with two groups of adoptive children. One includes adoptees born to a known child abuser. The other includes adoptees born to a normal adult. All our adoptees are brought up by loving adoptive parents. Upon reaching adulthood, all become parents, but what kind? To keep things simple, let's consider just two scenarios.

In the first, all our adoptees, including those born to abusers, prove to be good parents. Apparently, normal upbringing can suppress any genetic potential for abuse that might exist in some children. This, in turn, suggests that abusive rearing enhances any such abusive potential. Reasonable conclusion? *Parenting, not biology, is the major reason why some children become abusive parents.*

Sounds reasonable, but wait. We have a second scenario with a different outcome. Some of our adoptees born to abusive parents yet reared by normal parents nevertheless become abusive parents; yet none of our adoptees born of a normal adult does so. Now it seems, normal rearing *doesn't* suppress an abusive potential. Reasonable conclusion? *Biology, not parenting, is the major reason why some children become abusive parents.*

So then, which of these contrary conclusions is closer to the truth? Well, we still can't be sure because, sad to say, we still don't have adoption studies that focus on child abuse. Until we do, blaming abusive parents may seem reasonable, and surely satisfying, when we so despise such parents for their cruel and harmful behavior.

Yet simply blaming irresponsible parents for how their children turn out is at best a half truth if it turns out that special biological influences matter too. At worst, it is no truth at all if biological influences matter most. A safe guess, in my view, is that special biological influences do matter a lot. What else can explain why the *stepchildren* of child abusers are not especially likely to become abusive parents.

Comedian George Burns once quipped: "And God said: 'Let there be Satan, so people don't blame everything on me. And let there be lawyers, so people don't blame everything on Satan.'" I imagine God also saying: "And let there be twins and adoptees, so people don't blame everything on parents—even abusive parents." Amen!

We've explored the question of biological and social influences in family life. Yet what kind of question *is* it? It's scientific, yes, but social and moral as well. To see why, we need only consider expert opinions that have done much harm to good parents.

Expert opinion has traditionally favored social explanations for abnormal or otherwise deviant behavior. Obsessive-compulsive disorder, childhood autism, stuttering, homosexuality, depression, and suicide: All these supposedly arise primarily from deficient or defective parenting. Inborn factors are either ignored or minimized with brief lip service. Such notions about the primary role of poor parenting, we now know, are pure nonsense. Worse, they condemn parents without just cause.

For years, a social explanation of childhood autism was fashionable. Even medically trained psychiatrists spoke of "refrigerator mothers" whose cold, rejecting personality caused their child to become autistic. One such mother was told that she "had not connected or bonded with her child because of inability to properly relate to the child."

140

Never mind that her other children were not autistic. Never mind that any sensible person could see that mothers like her are typically anything but cold and rejecting. And never mind that truly cold, rejecting parents almost never have an autistic child. A mother asks: "What have we done that is so awful that would drive a child into such a regression?" The answer: Nothing. Autism is a brain disease. Parenting quality has nothing to do with it.

Most notorious of the parent blamers was Bruno Bettelheim, a one-time influential and widely quoted child therapist who was given to misdiagnosing and physically abusing his young charges and blaming parents for making their children mentally ill. In a revealing book, journalist Richard Pollak describes the frustration of being deceived and insulted by an apparent psychiatric charlatan. "My mother was the villain . . . almost entirely responsible for my brother's problems. With astonishing anger, he said she had rejected Stephen at birth and that to cope with this lockout he had developed 'pseudo-feeble-mindedness.'" It was just gobbledygook.

Most astounding is that for so long so many people thought Bettelheim was an authority on how parents cause their children to become autistic or schizophrenic. When Bettelheim committed suicide in 1990, *The Washington Post* celebrated "the originality, warmth and wisdom he brought to the study of the minds and emotions of children," while *The New York Times* noted that "he was widely admired as a practicing therapist and as a profound and original thinker in psychoanalysis." *Parenting* magazine suggested that Bettelheim "left to the world and especially to parents and children an enduring vision of love, innocence, and idealism."

Yet as columnist Joan Beck wrote, "The need to set the record straight about Bettelheim goes far beyond the fact that the famous guru who preached love and supportive care for children often beat them . . . and emotionally undermined them in ugly ways. It is important to discredit permanently Bettelheim's conviction that mental illness in children—especially autism—is caused by emotional factors, especially maternal feelings and behavior."

Likewise, for years, a social explanation of schizophrenia was fashionable. Even medically trained psychiatrists spoke of "schizophrenogenic mothers," mothers who *cause* schizophrenia by their poor parenting skills. Many people who should have known better continued to embrace this sorry notion even after 1966, the year it was thoroughly debunked by a spectacular finding.

At the time, psychiatrist Leonard Heston knew what many professionals knew. Children brought up by their schizophrenic mothers have a roughly 10 percent risk of developing the illness. That's *10 times greater* than what we would expect for other children.

But then Heston discovered something that few professionals even suspected. Children born to schizophrenic mothers but raised by adoptive parents have the *same* high 10-percent risk! Now there's even evidence that children born to normal parents but reared *by a schizophrenic parent* have the usual low risk for schizophrenia.

Apparently then, quality of parenting can't easily explain why children differ in their risk of developing schizophrenia when they grow up. Nor can it easily explain why the illness runs in some families but not others. Yet genetic and other inborn influences can easily explain both.

The findings of Heston and others were a wake-up call that many didn't hear and some chose to ignore. How sad, then, that for so long so many psychiatric professionals continued to blame parents for all sorts of mental illnesses afflicting their children. Does this kind of parent-blaming happen today? Apparently it does, as evident in this note written by the mother of a schizophrenic child.

The first psychiatrist we saw when our son dropped out of school and began screaming tirades against his parents diagnosed him as being in the throes of an adolescent revolt. I was a chaotic-thinking, intrusive mother; my husband was a rigid French father, and we abused our son emotionally by taking him to Europe. The fact that I had schizophrenia in my family didn't matter.

Heston's finding is a powerful reminder: *False social explanations can readily distract our attention from true biological causes, while causing grievous emotional harm.* We've seen the truth of this with abnormal as well as normal behavior. "Many emotional problems," says neuroscientist J. Allan Hobson, "stem from brain abnormalities masquerading as socially caused mental illness."

There are hundreds of thousands of [people] who have less dramatic but troublesome problems like anxiety, depression, and neurosis. Society readily assumes that all these people must have had some history of psychological stress or trauma that has caused them to be this way. I say no. They rant and rave, or flit about nervously, or fail to show up for work, or carry Valium in their purses because there is a functional disorder of . . . their brain-mind. They may well have been abused as children or have lost their self esteem, and this can cause real emotional distress. But it does not cause their actual anxiety, depression, neurosis, or any other of a long list of problems.

We now know that some mental illnesses are as medical as diabetes. Yet they often go unrecognized. In one study, for example, almost half the people referred for psychiatric treatment proved to have a medical condition. In some cases, the medical condition was causing the mental illness. In others, it was complicating the mental illness.

An unsuspected brain disorder, for example, can cause disordered thinking or severe depression or violent behavior. It can make one person strangely humorless or moralistic. It can make another endlessly dwell on minor details or go off on irrelevant tangents. It can make a third person become overwhelmed by even trivial things that seem to have deep philosophical meaning.

We may view such peculiar behavior as merely eccentric or oddball. We might speculate about its deep roots in early childhood experience. We may blame the parents. Yet the truth can lie elsewhere.

143

During an interview with a neurologist, an absent-minded professor was describing a peculiar incident involving his oddly destructive driving habits. Suddenly his exasperated wife chimed in:

Well Robert, there was a lot more to it than that. You drove in reverse down a line of three parked cars and ignored my calls to stop. Then you put the car in forward and drove for two more blocks—and through a stop sign. I was frantic and begged you to stop, but you completely ignored me. After I asked you for the tenth time to pull over, you finally looked at me and turned into the gardening store's parking lot. When I showed you the damage to our car and said that we had to go back and leave a note for the people whose cars you'd hit, all you could say was, "Whatever pleases you."

For many years, Robert had exhibited occasional episodes of similar odd behavior. At a faculty dinner years earlier, he had mumbled something unintelligible. Moments later, he leaned forward until his face lay in his food. Many assumed that Robert's behavior was from too much drinking. Yet Robert had downed only a couple of drinks. Some might have wondered if Robert didn't have a just a little problem with attitude and upbringing. Few suspected the truth, that his eccentric behaviors arose from a treatable brain disorder.

Stories about mental illness can illuminate deep truths about family life and child development. How then should we view social theories that seem plausible to parents yet confuse or obscure important biological reasons why our children turn out the way they do? I suggest we keep a clear eye on the ball, I mean the ball of solid scientific findings that give us real answers to the toughest questions we can ask about our kids and ourselves.

Let's say we still believe that even normal differences in parenting can make a big a difference to how kids turn out—that our way of parenting can make a big difference to how *our* kids turn out. And we know that many experts agree, some even embracing the idea with what seems like religious fervor.

Well, I've been arguing that we parents need cold evidence, not hot feelings. We need *credible* answers to difficult questions. Easy questions are, well, easy and their easy answers don't get us far. Worse, they can delude us into thinking we know something important when actually we don't. With such false or misleading answers, we are worse off than we would be without them.

Both "nature" and "nurture" can easily explain why parents and their children show similarities in personality and behavior. Sure, but can both provide credible answers to the really hard questions? Here are six such questions, most of which we've considered throughout this book.

• Why are identical twins who grow up apart so similar in so many ways as identicals who grow up together?

• Why are adoptively related siblings who grow up together so different, in some ways as different as strangers?

• Why are adopted children more like the biological parents they've never known than the adoptive parents who raised them?

• Why are the children of bright parents generally somewhat less bright than their parents while the children of dull parents are generally somewhat less dull than their parents?

• Why do bright children generally have somewhat less bright parents while dull children generally have somewhat less dull parents?

• Why do some children reared by good or even super parents nevertheless wind up doing badly in life, while some reared by irresponsible or even abusive parents wind up doing well?

We need convincing answers to *all* these difficult questions. Where can we find such answers? Clearly not in the usual "nurture views" offered up in the nightly TV news, TV interview shows, or weekly news magazines. Rather, we can find them in "nature views" such as the one we've been exploring together. That's why I have been suggesting we put aside any negative feelings we may have about the power of "nature," keep an open mind, and ask the obvious question. Which view should we prefer: one that can answer *all* those hard questions or one that can't?

With this key question in mind, try a little experiment that anyone can do. Just cozy up to a newborn baby and, with a big smile and nodding head, wiggle your tongue from side to side.

What happens next is both cute and quite wonderful. After staring at you intently, the newborn should begin imitating your wiggly tongue! Sure, the infant's wiggle may be awkward or goofy. No matter. It happens and more to the point, it happens without benefit of prior experience or parental instruction. Somehow, infants "translate" a wiggly tongue they can barely see "out there" (whatever *that* means) into a responsive wiggle.

Clearly the infant's "genius" for appreciating a wiggly tongue is innate, in the tissue and not in the teaching. Likewise, I've been saying, much of an infant's potential "genius" for personal development, including a "genius" for doing good or evil, resides in the tissue and not in the teaching.

Rooted within, it unfolds, ripening from within with impressive persistence however influenced it may be by the "out there" of social life. That is why, without considering tissue as well as teaching, we can hardly appreciate or ever really understand why our children turn out the way they do.

Goldberger's heroic experiments proved that one "sure thing" really wasn't so sure after all. The lesson in his story is that we can never be too careful with "sure things." As any magician can tell you, what you see may *not* be what you get when you look a little closer. Take a look at these little "arrows."

The shaft of the upper one looks longer but is really shorter; the shaft of the lower one looks shorter but is really longer. Even

after closer inspection, the longer shaft still looks shorter, and the shorter one still looks longer.

Yet how often do we bother to look closely when it comes to our real-life beliefs? Let's say we do bother, but consider only those things we care about. Then how do we know if what we are *not* considering isn't as important or even more important? It surely was important for Mrs. Coolidge, at least according to legend.

Soon after arriving at a government farm, President and Mrs. Coolidge were taken on separate tours. When Mrs. Coolidge passed the chicken pens she asked if the rooster copulates more than once a day. "Dozens of times," the man in charge replied. "Please tell that to the president," she said. When the president passed the pens and was told the same thing about the rooster, he asked if it was the same hen each time. "Oh no, Mr. President, a different one each time." The president nodded knowingly and said, "Please tell that to Mrs. Coolidge."

Clearly, which questions we ask or fail to ask will depend on our biases. Yet Francis Bacon had it right when he said: "Whatever the mind seizes with peculiar satisfaction is to be held in suspicion . . . ." And that means having an open mind and a willingness to question our assumptions, especially about our children and ourselves.

Conclusion
A Clear Message

Does our biology really have so much influence on our destiny? Let's say we can't help being less intelligent or sociable, or more moody or antisocial, than other people are. Do our problems and our resistance to change reflect a stronger influence of biology than we ever suspected? If it is so, then it must likewise be so for our abilities to manage those problems. Biological influence is as much about what is noble in us as what is base.

The alcoholic is not responsible for his disease. Yet despite a tougher row to hoe, he is still responsible—even more responsible than the rest of us—for avoiding drink. The epileptic is not responsible for her disease. Yet, she is even more responsible than the rest of us for any decision to drive that puts others at risk.

Each of us must try to behave well even when the "bad" parts of our biology push us to behave otherwise. This means digging deep for our "good" parts. Likewise, each of us must try to help our children behave well even when the "bad" parts of their biology push them to behave otherwise. This means helping them dig deep for their "good" parts.

We parents *can* make a difference in how our children turn out, their biology permitting. An absolutely wonderful story shared with me by Albert, an unusually insightful college student bears testimony to this.

During my childhood, I realized that I was different from the other kids. None of my friends suffered from panic attacks when their parents dropped them off at school. In this and in other ways, I was certainly the oddball. I was a good artist, an intuitive and deep thinker with a good sense of humor. These qualities and my eccentricities served as indicators of my giftedness. Even so, I was suffering from a pervasive anxiety disorder.

I have had Obsessive-Compulsive Disorder [OCD] since I was five years old, and it is difficult to convey how much this condition has affected my life. I remember the elaborate rituals that consumed my childhood. One involved five daily laps around the bike racks to ensure my parents would make it safely home. Another involved making sure that the water jug in the refrigerator faced just the right way.

I remember blaming my parents for my distress. I was embarrassed and needed to blame someone. Looking back, I realize that my parents weren't to blame. Only now do I realize that my condition was determined before I left the womb. Truth is, I was extremely lucky to have the parents I had. Both were too well educated on mental illness to abide by the popular habit of hiding their child's illness. Rather they simply provided the care and support I needed to seek treatment. They realized that childhood OCD, much like diabetes, has a strong genetic component and that it isn't the result of faulty rearing. How ironic that many people still believe poor parenting is a big cause of mental illness, when in reality, poor parenting is the cause of delaying treatment.

Now, as I embark on a medical education, I am more aware than ever of what it means to be a good parent. Such parents respect their child's natural tendencies while recognizing the limited extent of their influence. After all, my parents didn't cause my OCD anymore than they caused me to have brown eyes.

This lovely story is about behavior and character. It's about childhood memories and feelings. Most touchingly, it's about appreciation of parents. It conveys the same message I've offered throughout this book. We are responsible for providing quality parenting that combines love with discipline to encourage the best and suppress the worst in our children. Still, we must appreciate that there are strict limits to what we can accomplish. That means even our best efforts can carry no guarantees for how things turn out.

To understand the outcome of games, we must understand the rules. Likewise with the outcome of parenting, we must understand its rules, specifically the Big Five, that restate and summarize all we have explored in earlier chapters.

Rule 1 *Good parenting means helping children become civilized and socially responsible.*

Good parenting works to civilize the dark forces of human nature. It's the fine art of managing behavior so that we can protect our children not just from physical or social harm, but from themselves. This means managing behavior in the home but where possible, managing a child's choice of peers who can strongly influence a child's behavior for better or worse.

With that fine art firmly in place, our children have their best chance to develop a sense of responsibility for their behavior and a firmer sense of who they are and what they stand for. Without it, they become far more selfish, immature, and antisocial than they would otherwise have been.

Rewards and punishments wisely given show how much that parents are emotionally engaged with their children. Normally, these interventions help children learn the art of negotiation by which they come to appreciate the difference between what is permissible and what is not. A family environment need not be peaceful. It need only be reasonably safe so that conflict and other unpleasantness can be sensibly resolved.

Rule 2 *Good parenting means respecting children, not just loving them.*

Every child needs love and respect, for respect without love is mere cold comfort, while love without respect is mere warm illusion. Much of a parent's success will depend on how well or poorly we handle major concerns and worries that every child has about the following:

150

• Challenging situations that involve, for instance, sibling rivalry, parental conflict, parental drug use, or peer pressure to get involved with drugs and sexual performance, which can be especially anxiety-provoking and potentially traumatizing for young girls;

• Emotional stress involving anxiety, envy, anger, despair;

• Self-confidence, especially when threatened by doubts about being able to compete successfully with siblings or peers, fit in socially, and perform academically;

• Personality and personality changes involving, on the one hand, secretiveness about worries and on the other hand, emotional turmoil, possibly along with emotional withdrawal, hostility, and apparent inability to understand, let alone appreciate, how irrational and destructive such behavior really is;

• Moral questions involving honesty, loyalty, obligation, entitlement, justice, honor, especially when situations that stimulate the worst of human nature urge just the opposite: dishonesty, disloyalty, and dishonor through self-indulgent, self-centered behavior. Such conflict between "good" and "bad" is much more likely to affect our children when our behavior—for instance, tax cheating, irresponsible driving, recreational drug-taking—or their school's curriculum—for instance, which explores and even seems to condone sexual activity—contradicts our fine words about right and wrong; and finally

• Ultimate questions about life, death, and God.

Wise parents understand that children may at times seem delusional, even "crazy." Nevertheless, they can take small comfort in knowing that, however secretive or resentful they may be, such children do hear and hold in their memory what parents share in an urgent, yet loving, non-accusatory manner, and that deep down, their children really do find comfort in knowing that their parents can be trusted and that they really do care. It's the kind of realization that can affect in a positive way lifetime thoughts and feelings about a parent and about family relationships.

At the same time, wise parents show respect for their children by continuing to encourage their best instincts and evident talents, say in art, music, science, or sport, with opportunities and encouragement. They know it may take a variety of experiences before some possible hidden ability or talent is finally triggered. They also know that their efforts can be ruined by distractions from peers and from their children's own newly developing sexual impulses and need for autonomy and social acceptance. Finally, they know not to push children beyond their abilities, and to ease off when they recognize that a talent just isn't there.

Children are not mini-replicas of their parents. They may feel pressure to conform to parental hopes and dreams. They may even identify with these, at least for a while. Yet eventually, they have little choice but to follow their own psychological paths, despite what we parents try to make them do. Still, our children must learn what is expected of them while they learn to be themselves. Wise parents are therefore attentive and caring, yet encourage their own and society's reasonable expectations.

Perhaps most difficult of all, we parents must learn when it is time to let go, even when our emotions say hang on. Over the years, our children naturally tend to move away from us, psychologically and physically. Most do so despite their love and loyalty. Smart parents understand this biological fact of social life. Wise parents embrace it or at least resign themselves to it.

Everything we do, if truly in a child's interest, should foster natural competencies for independent and autonomous growth. Parents can accomplish only so much, yet with a little luck and hard work, sometimes more than they dared to hope.

Rule 3 *Parents have limited ability to predict their child's development.*

Predicting how a child will turn out is hazardous at best. The roll of genetic "dice" can make our children quite different from what we expected. We can see this inner fact of life in the extraordinary offspring—great leaders, creative geniuses, psychotics—of ordinary parents. We can see it in the ordinary offspring of extraordinary parents. Finally, we can see it in dramatic changes children display as they grow into adults. After a stormy beginning, a problem child becomes a happy, productive adult. After an uneventful beginning, a seemingly normal child becomes mentally ill. It's a fact of life. Despite their hopes and expectations, despite their best efforts, parents will often wind up being surprised at how things turn out.

Rule 4 *Parents have limited ability to control their child's psychological destiny.*

Normally, parents can do little to transform personality, improve intelligence, or create character. Much of what our children learn need not follow from what they see or from what we try to teach them. Even with good parenting, our children may still be insecure, uninspired, unfulfilled, rebellious. They may be so burdened with mental or emotional disability, a parent can do relatively little, even with the help of therapy or special education. Yet even with bad parenting, most children have the inner resiliency to resist or at least bounce back. The mistakes most parents make will in all likelihood normally have no more lasting effect than a bruise that leaves no scar.

Some parental influence is short-lived because children naturally slough off what lacks personal relevance. *Other parental influence is long-lived yet depends on the child, that is, a natural receptivity to such influence that may or may not be there.* If not, that parental influence may have unforeseen consequences.

Demanding good conduct may work for a while. Likewise, harping on the virtues of hard work and good study habits may work for a while. Yet such urgings may backfire. Demands for high achievement may alienate a bright but vulnerable, headstrong, or unambitious child. In short, even where we do have some influence, the effects may not be what we expected or intended.

Finally, *some parental influence is simply illusory.* It reflects not what we parents have done or failed to do but the genes we share with our children.

Rule 5 *Parents have limited moral responsibility for how a child turns out.*

We parents need to lighten up! Much of what happens, the good as well as the bad, will happen regardless of what we normally do. The reason is simple enough. No one—neither we nor our child—has ultimate control over genetic, prenatal, and social factors outside the family that determine what we are and what we become. That means we must try to distinguish our real influence from the illusory kind. It also means we must take less blame for our "failures" but also less credit for our "triumphs."

By taking too much credit or blame, we deny our children's unique genius for self-determination. By taking too much credit or blame, we also deny their power to influence our behavior, and therefore any influence we may have on their development. Finally, by taking too much credit or blame, we deny their own successes or failures, which can minimize their personal responsibility.

We can likewise assume that our parents had the same powers over us. But doesn't assuming so deny our own inner genius for self-determination? Don't we thereby deny the reality of our own successes or failures, while we minimize our own personal responsibility? Hopefully, our parents had no such power over us and neither do we over our children. A good thing too, for only with a unique individuality that springs from within can we and our children truly be our own persons. Only in such individuality can there be true human dignity for us all.